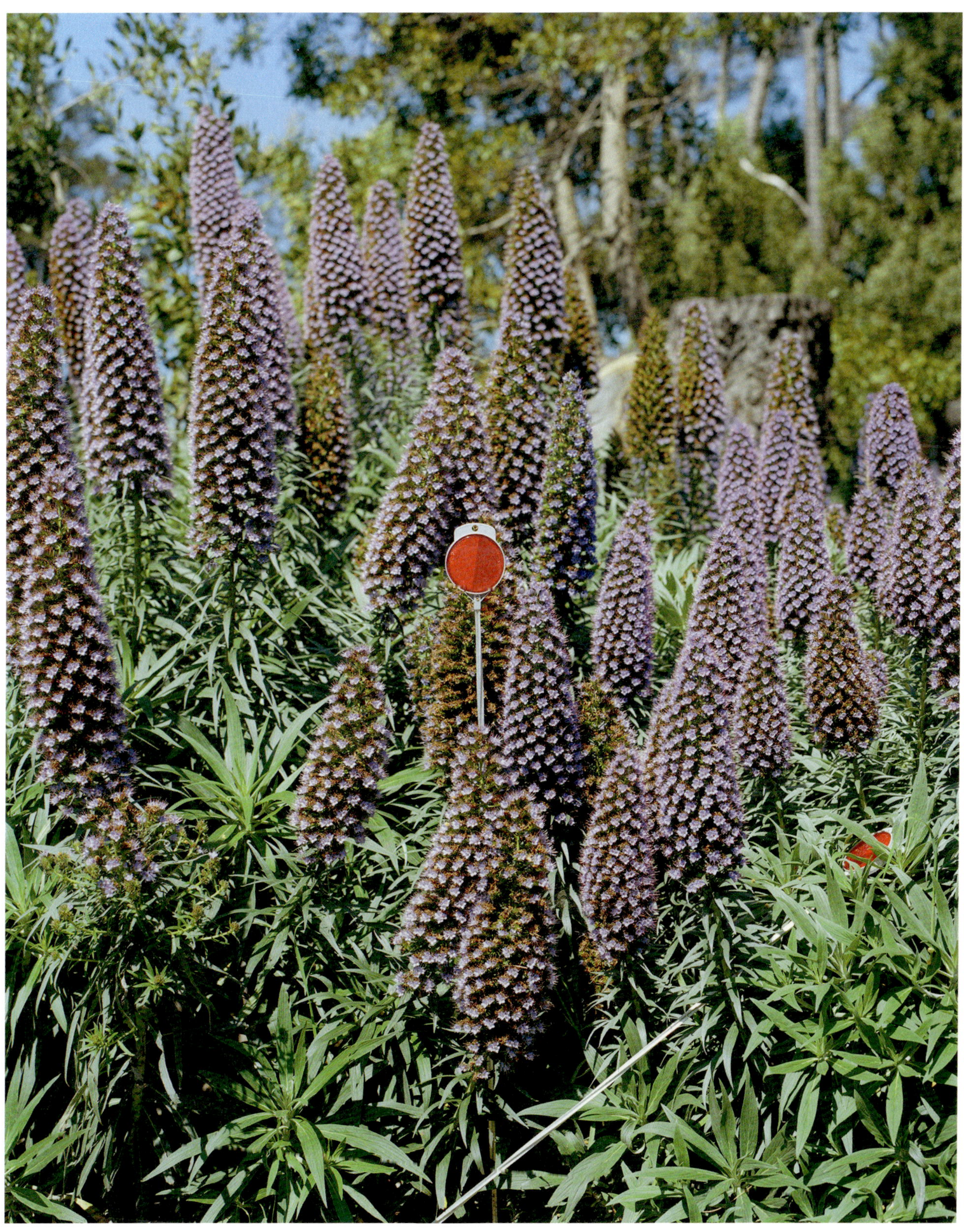

dana stirling

why am i sad

KEHRER

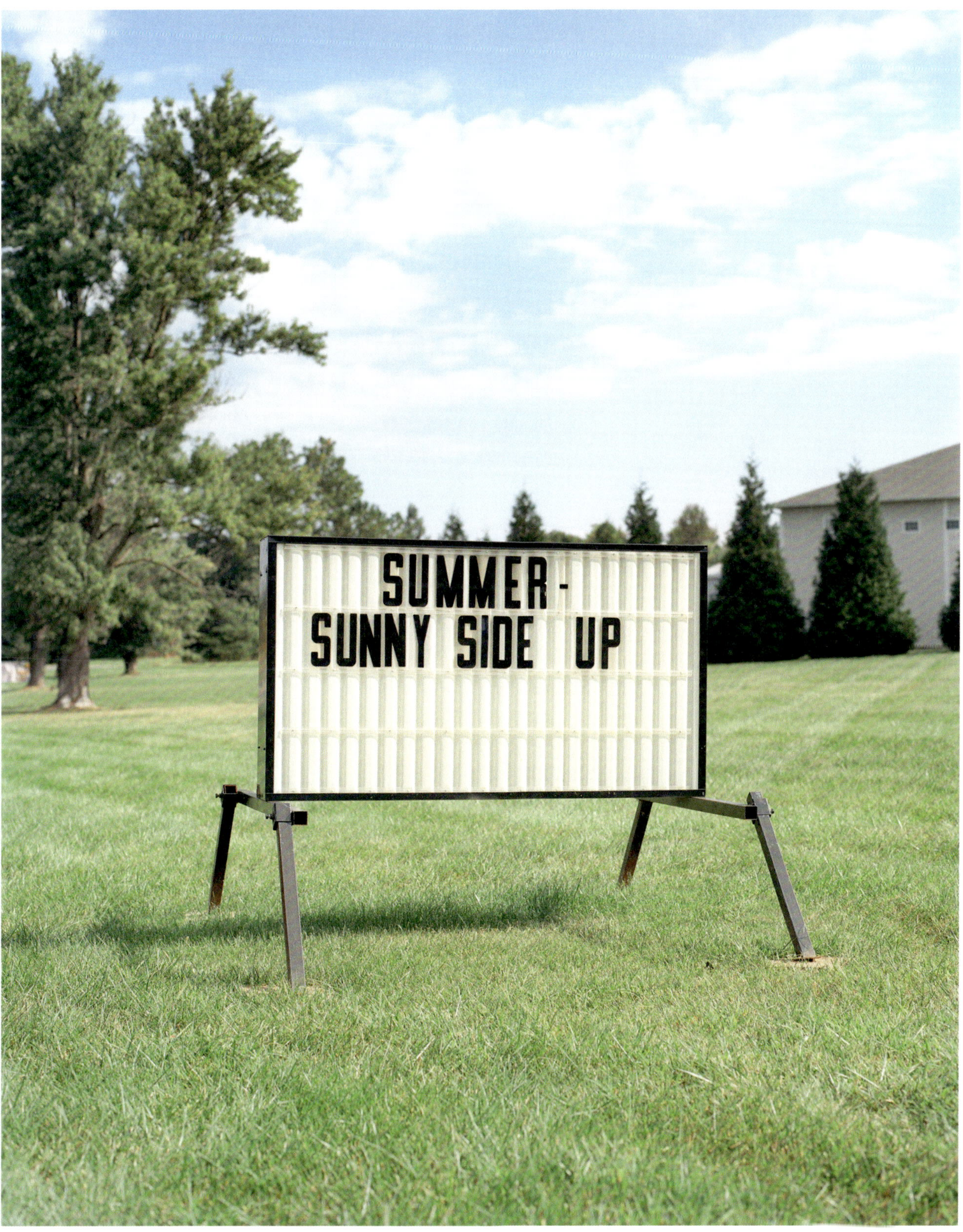
SUMMER -
SUNNY SIDE UP

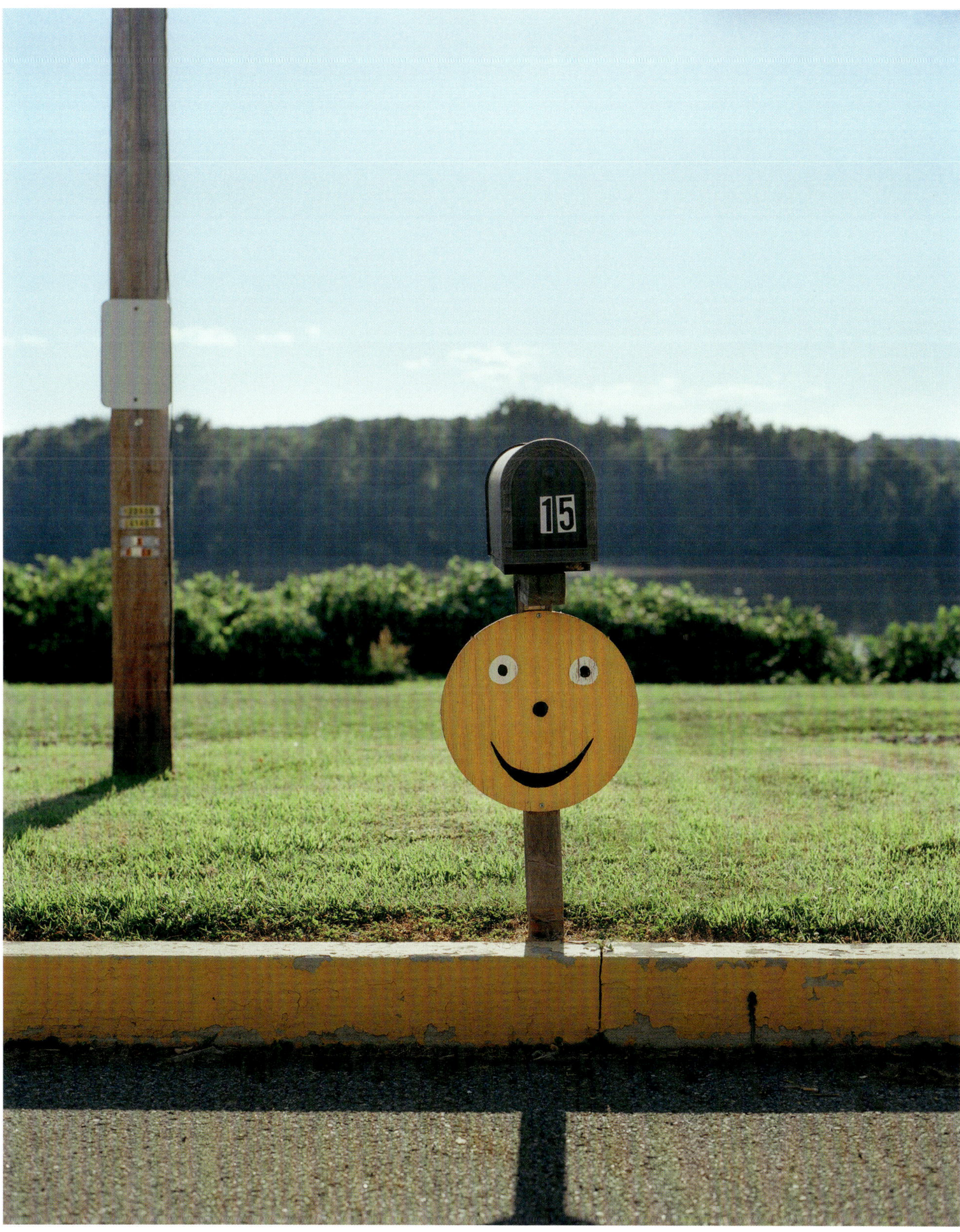
15

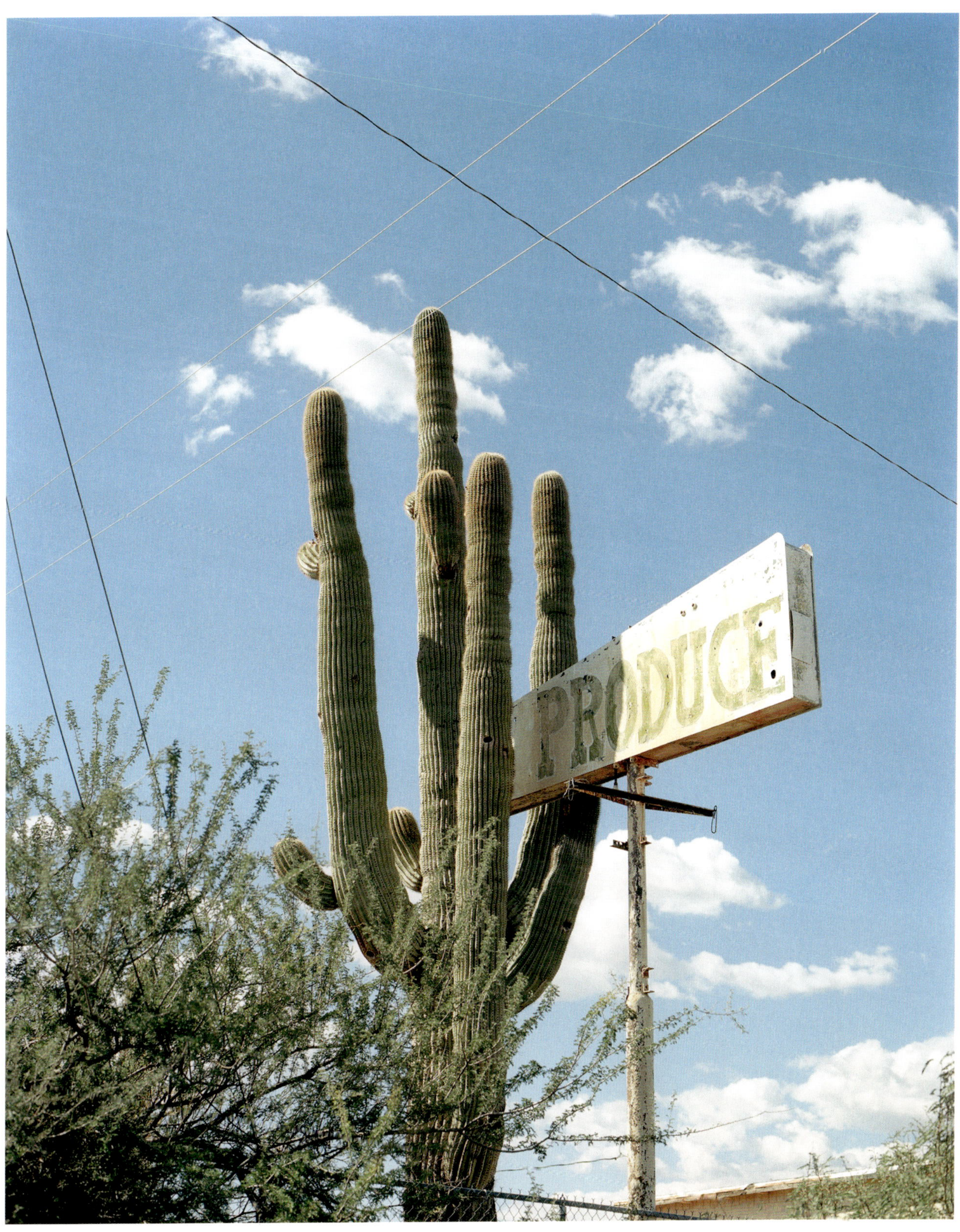
PRODUCE

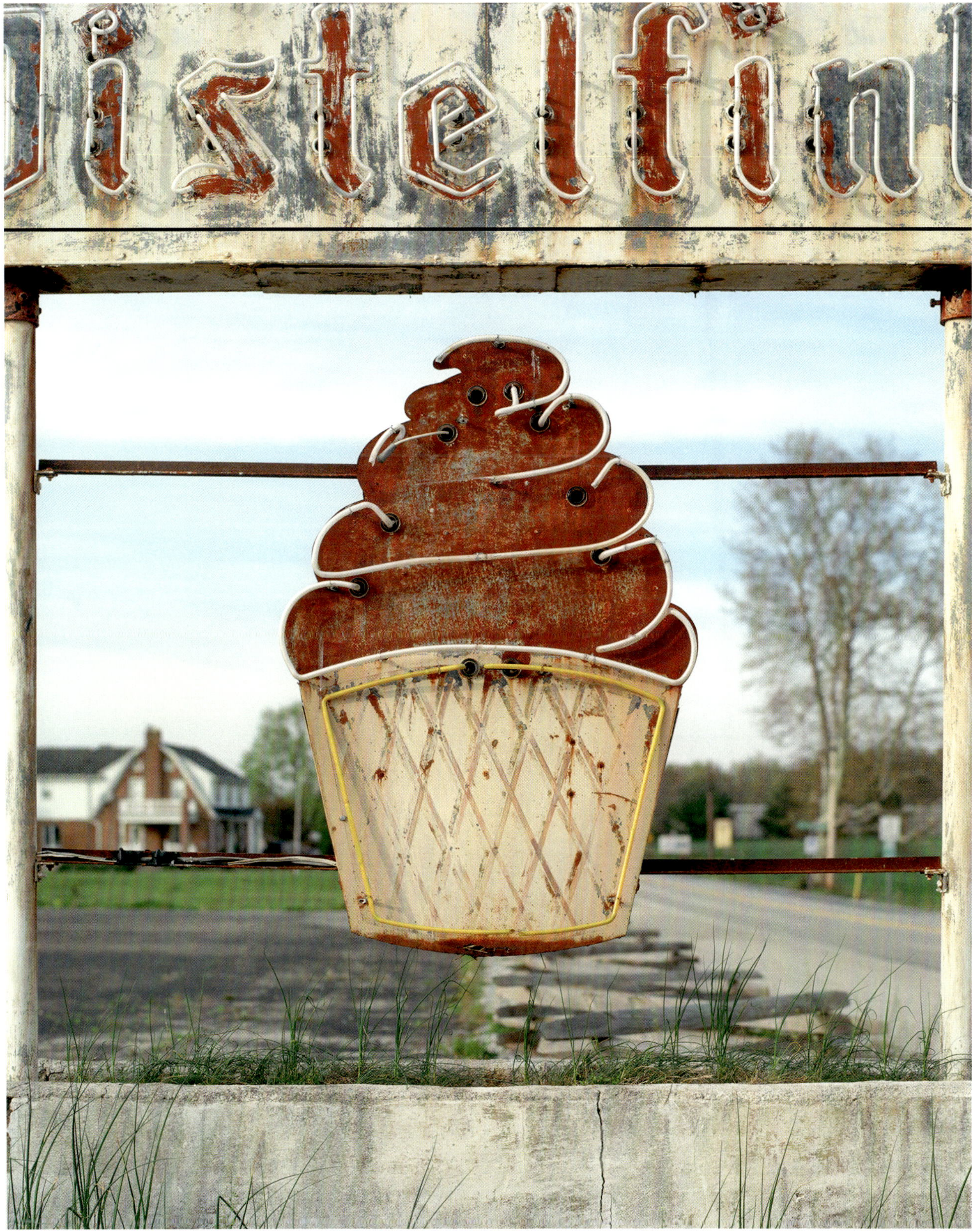
istelfin

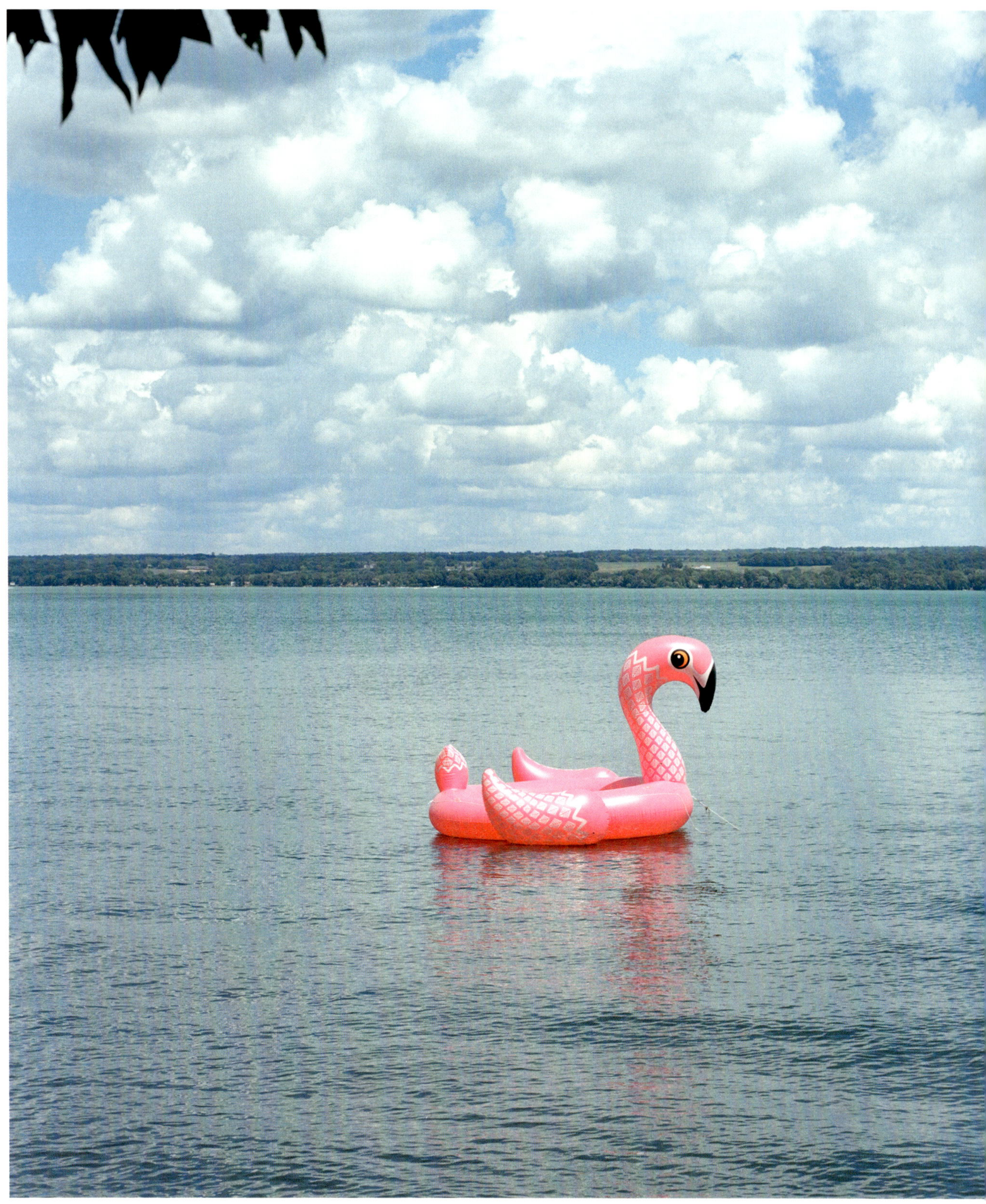

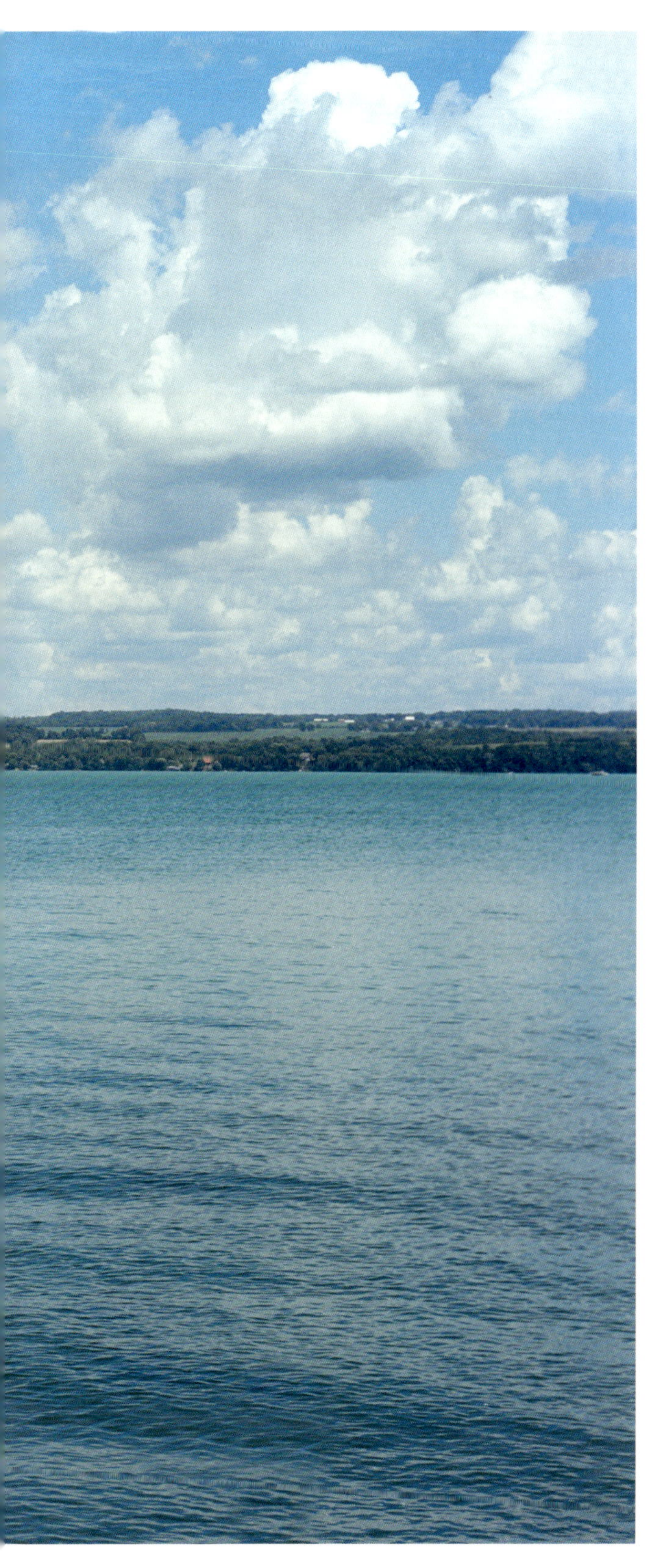

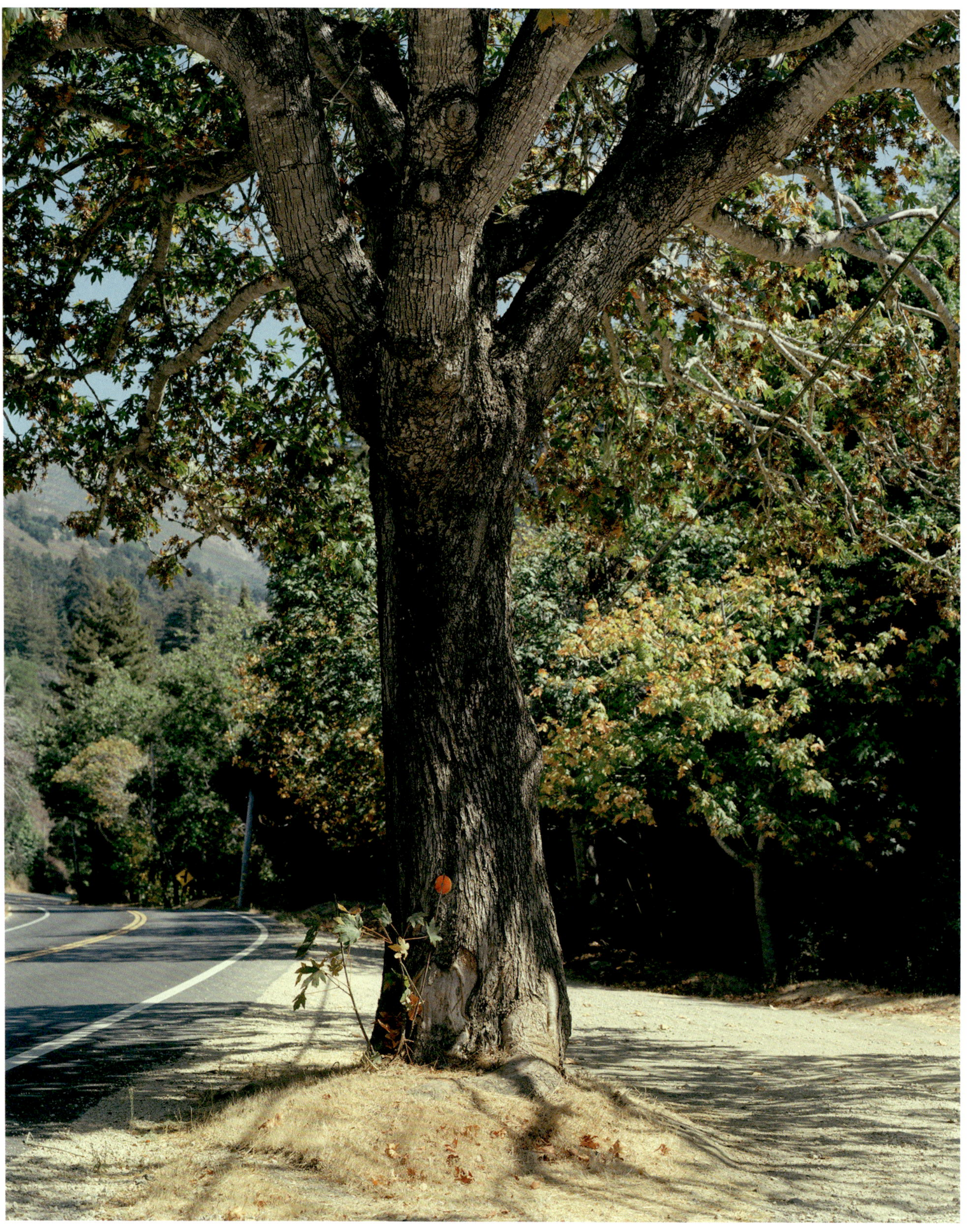

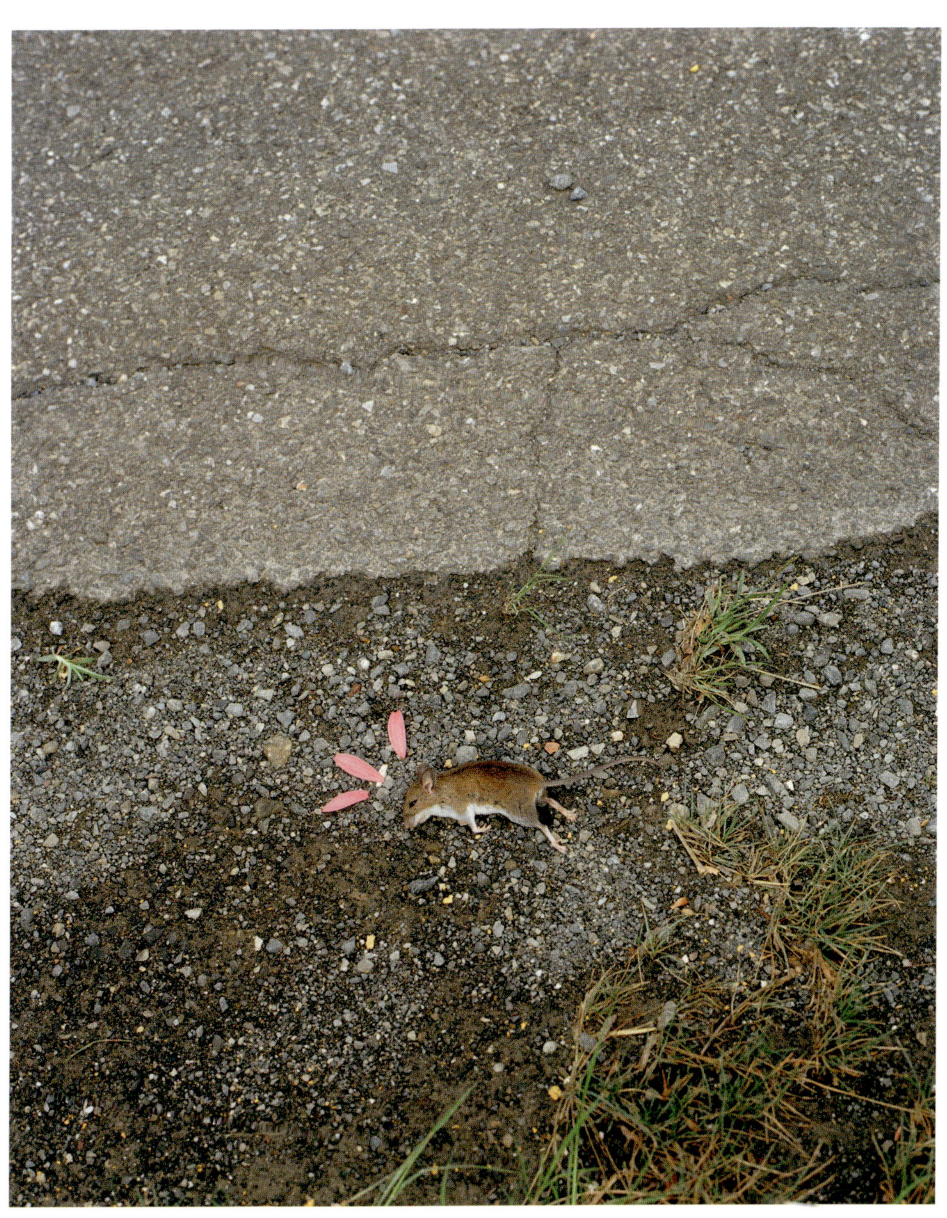

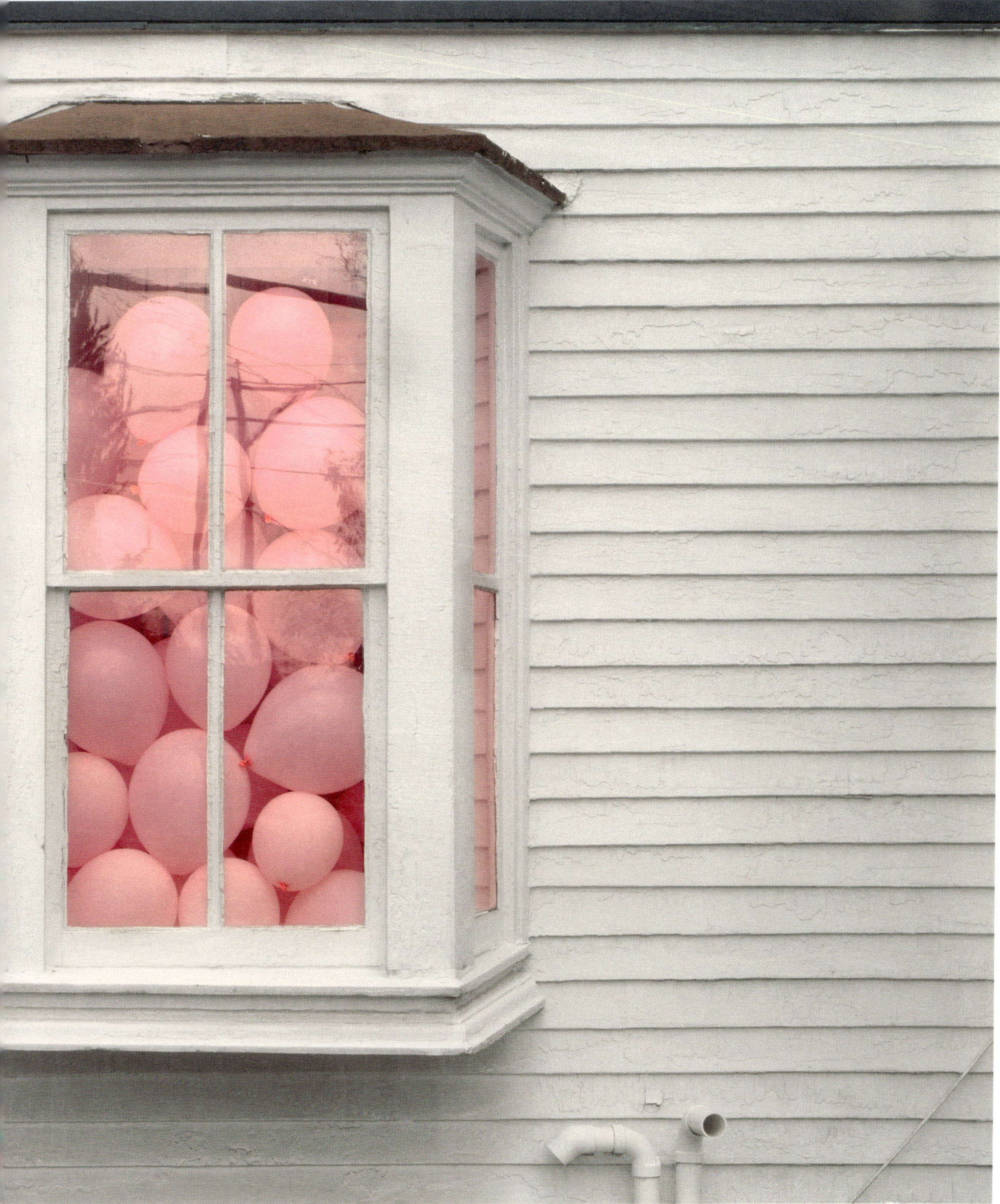

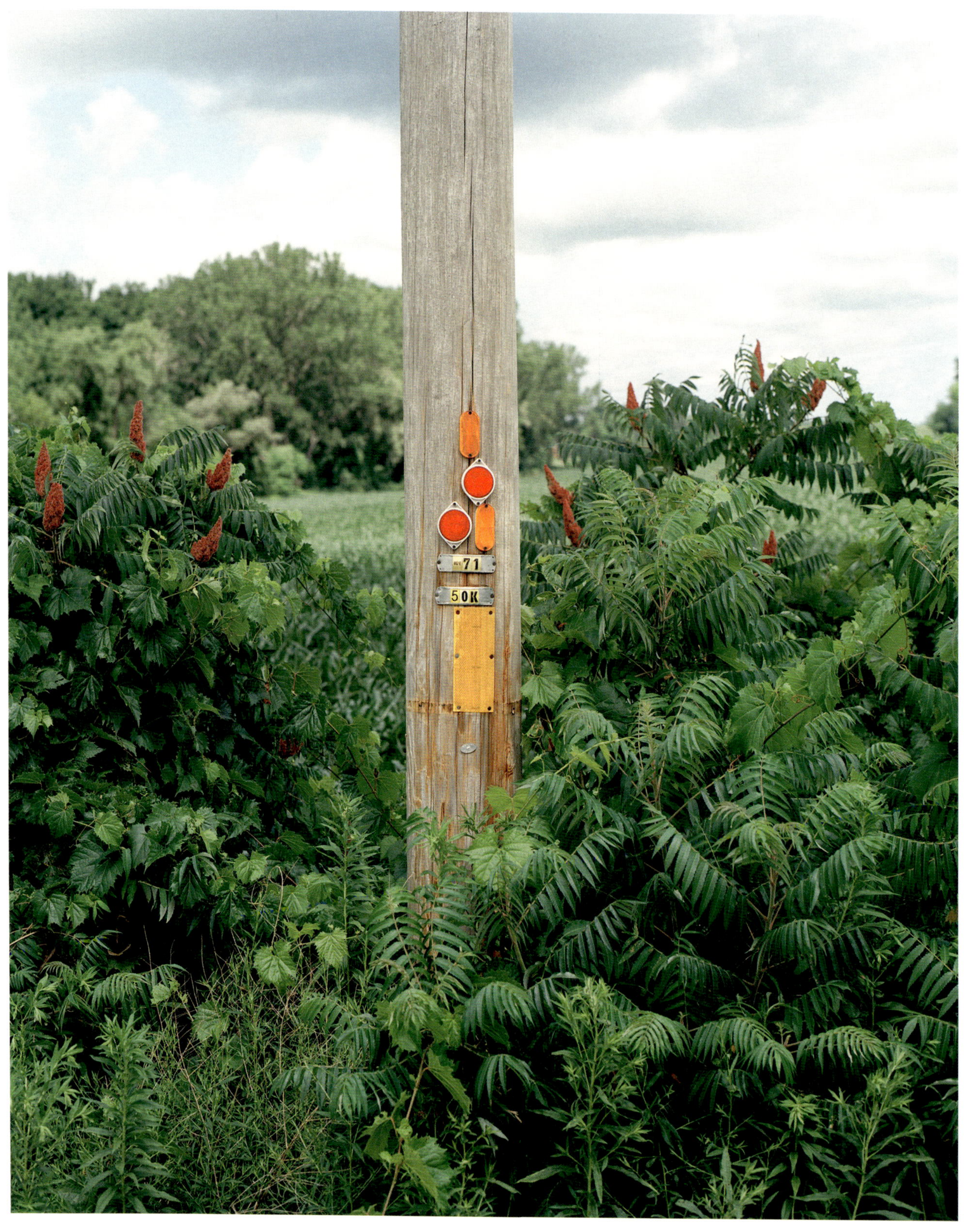
71
50K

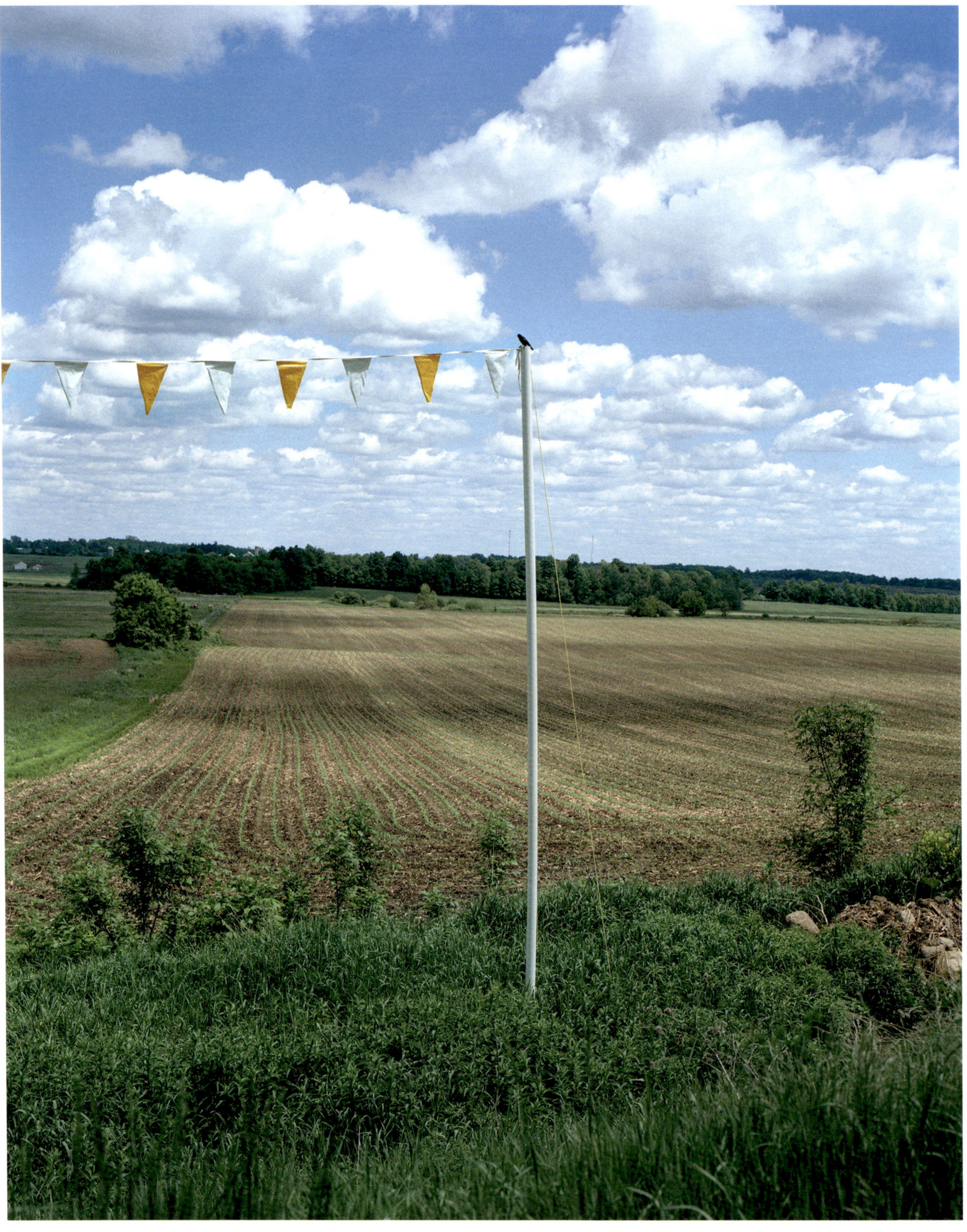

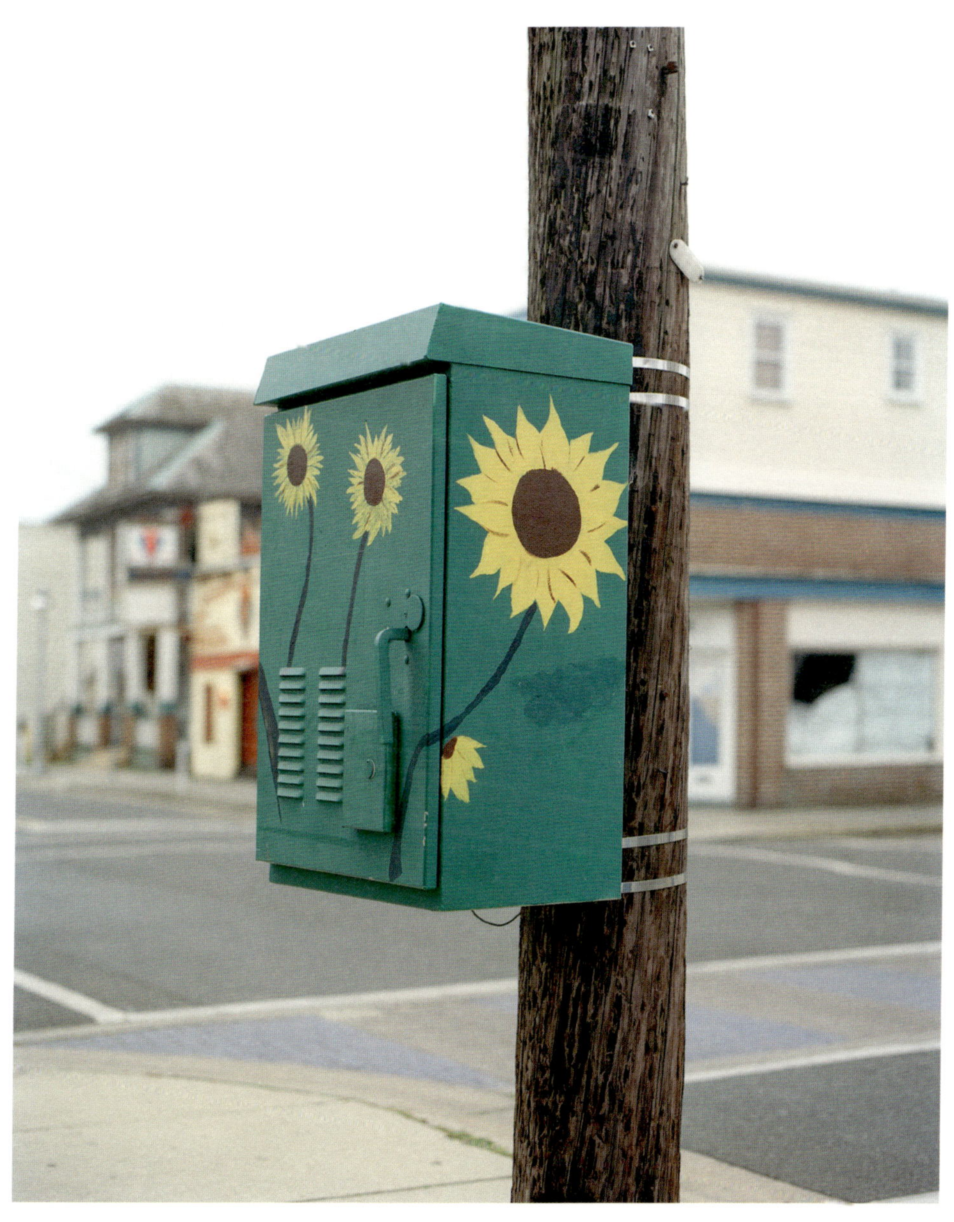

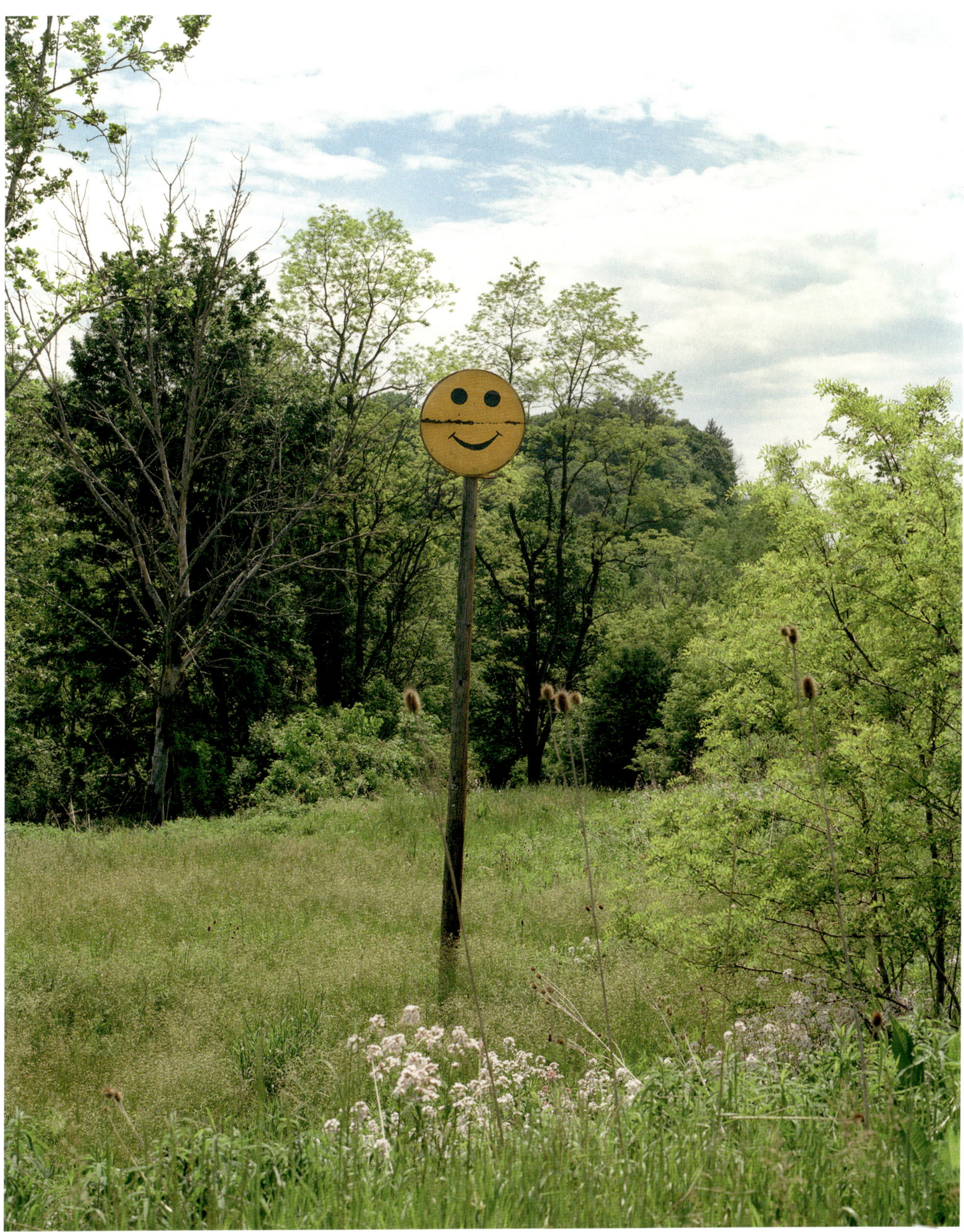

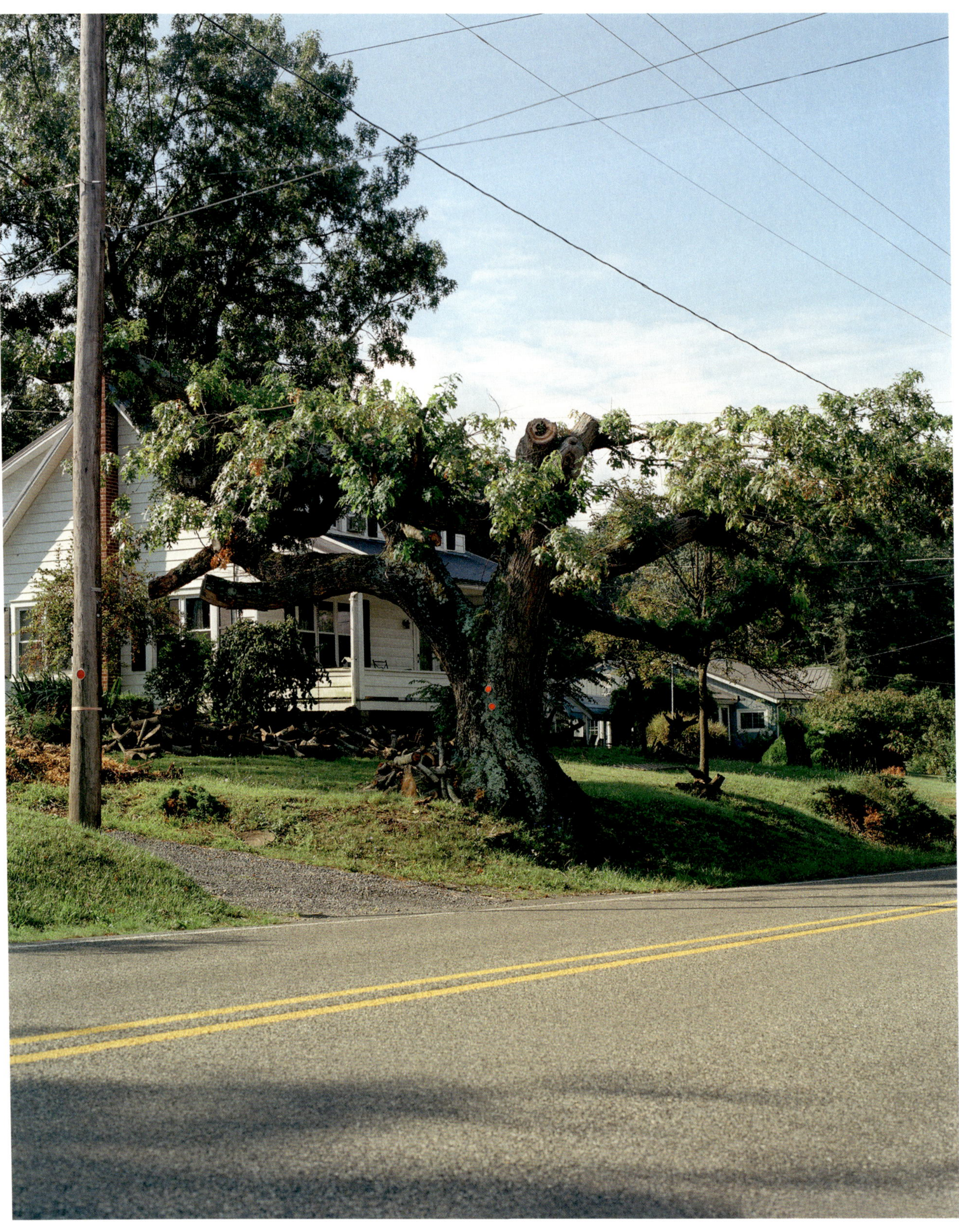

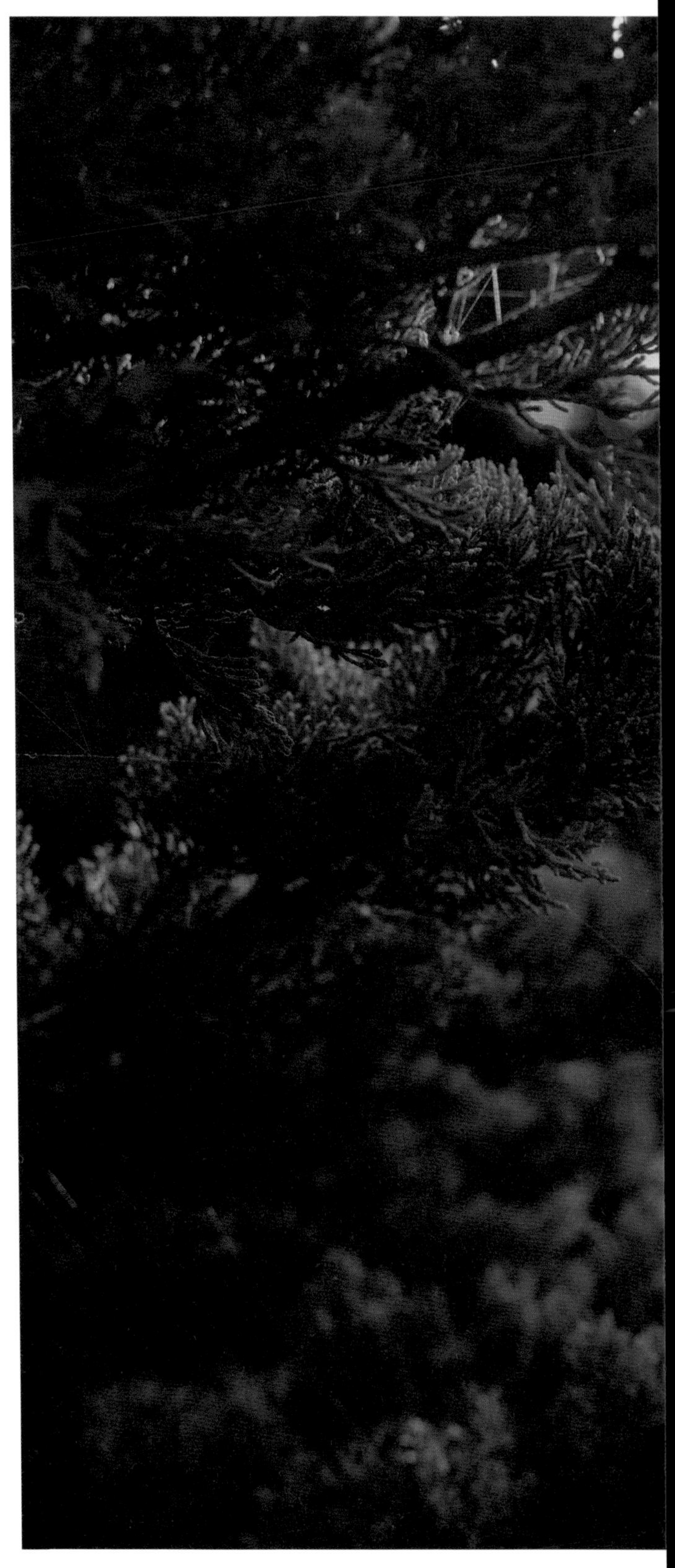

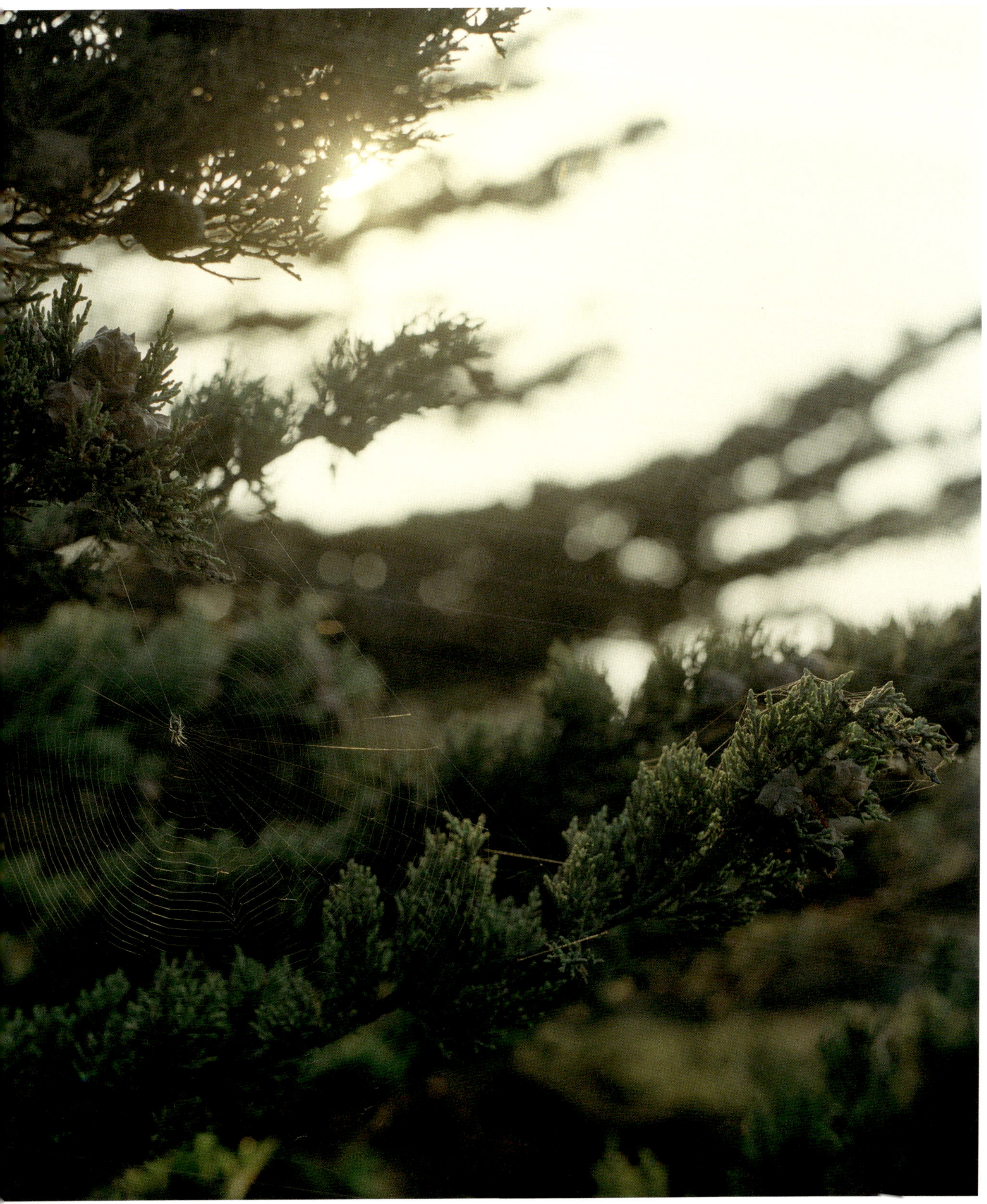

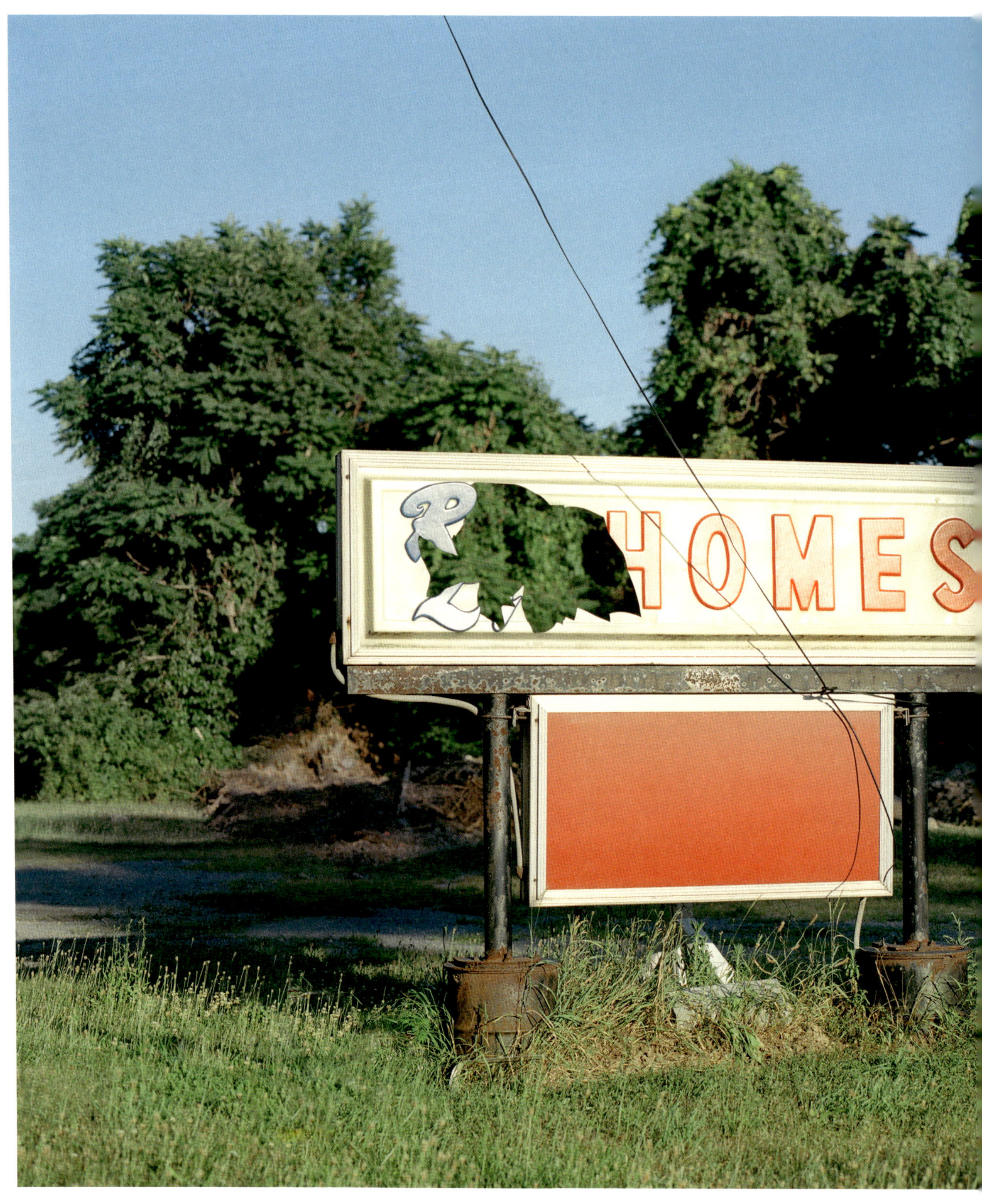
HOMES

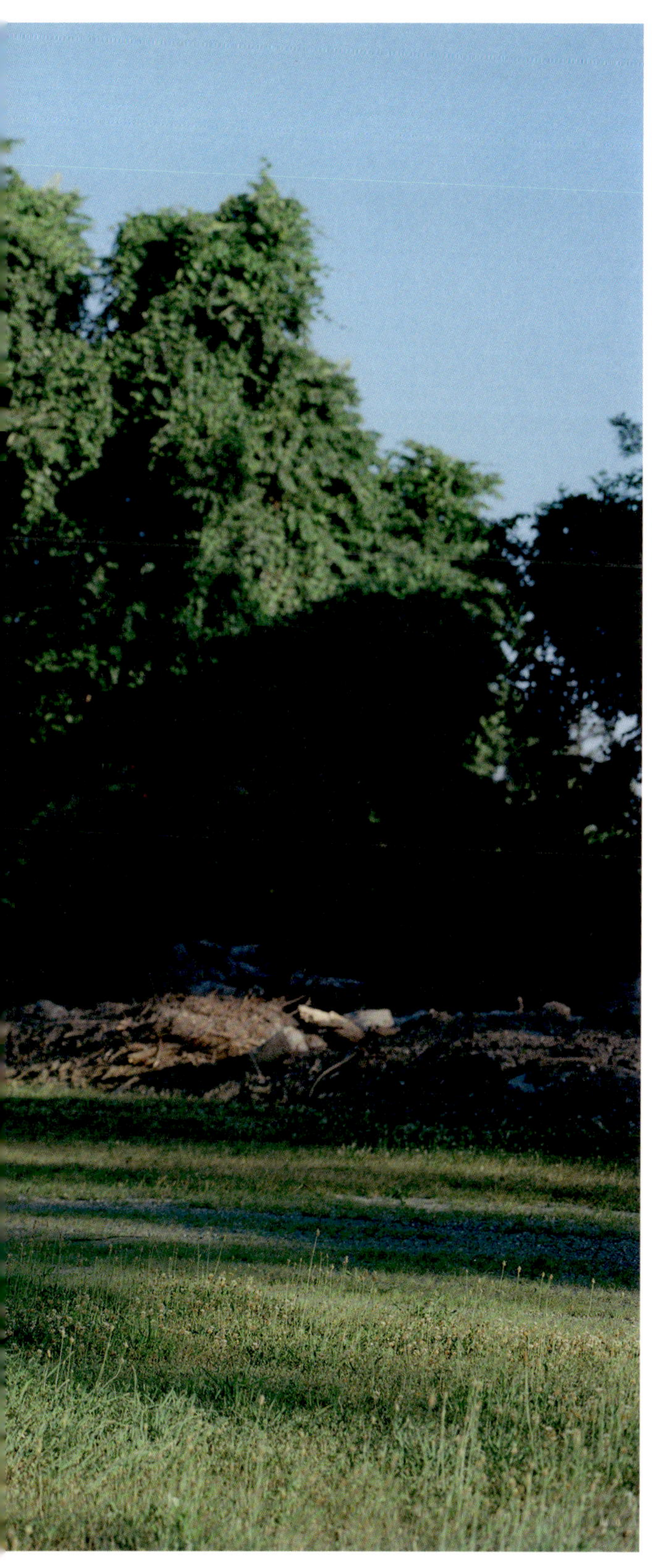

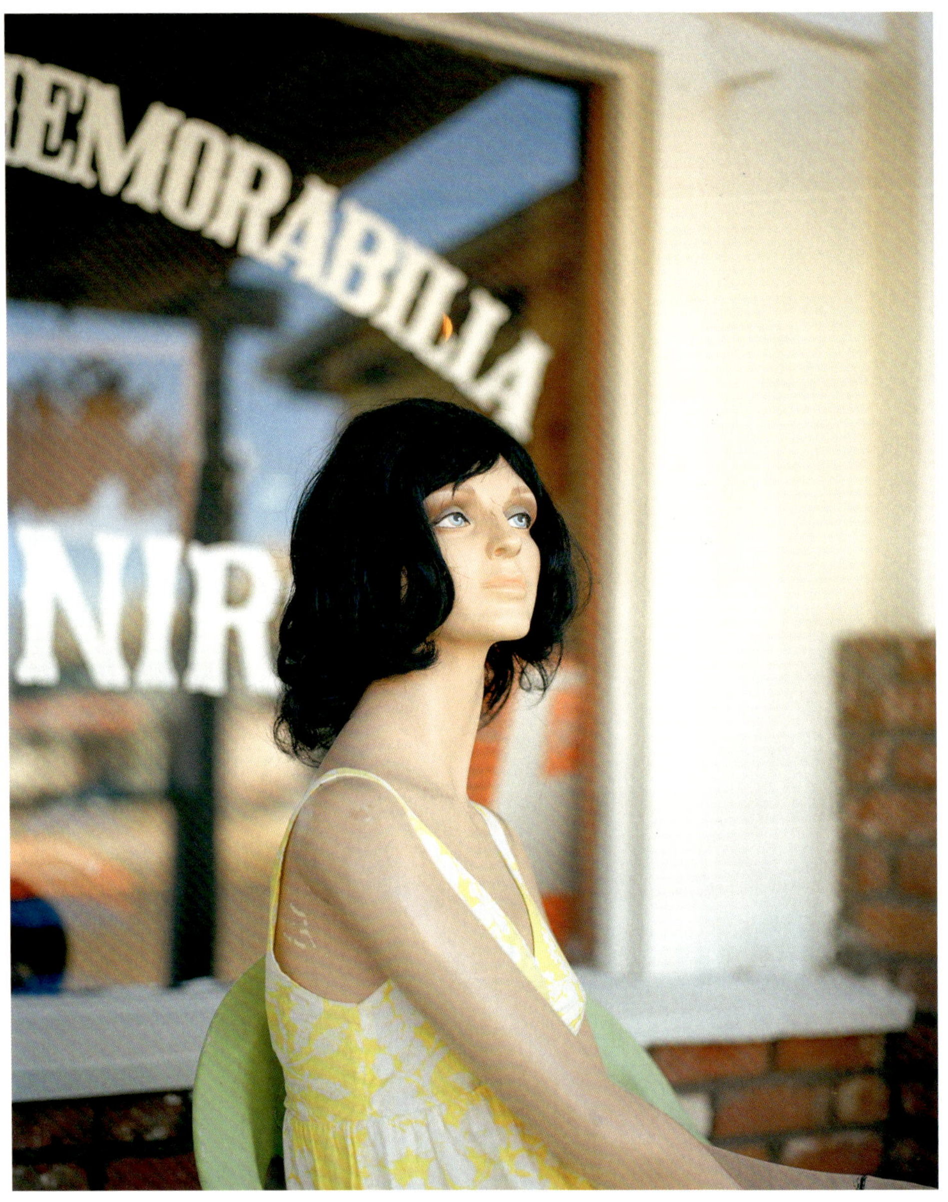
EMORABILIA
NIR

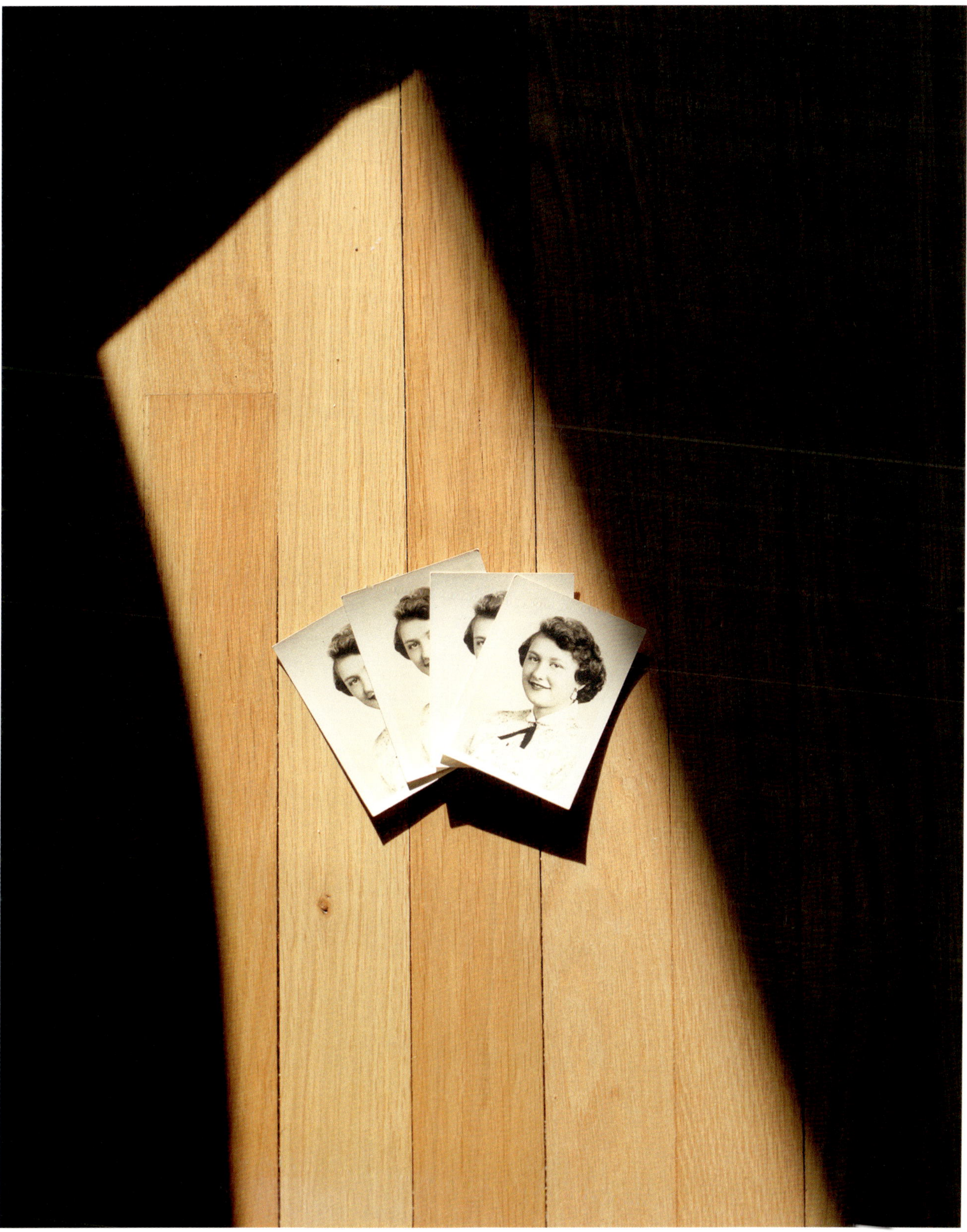

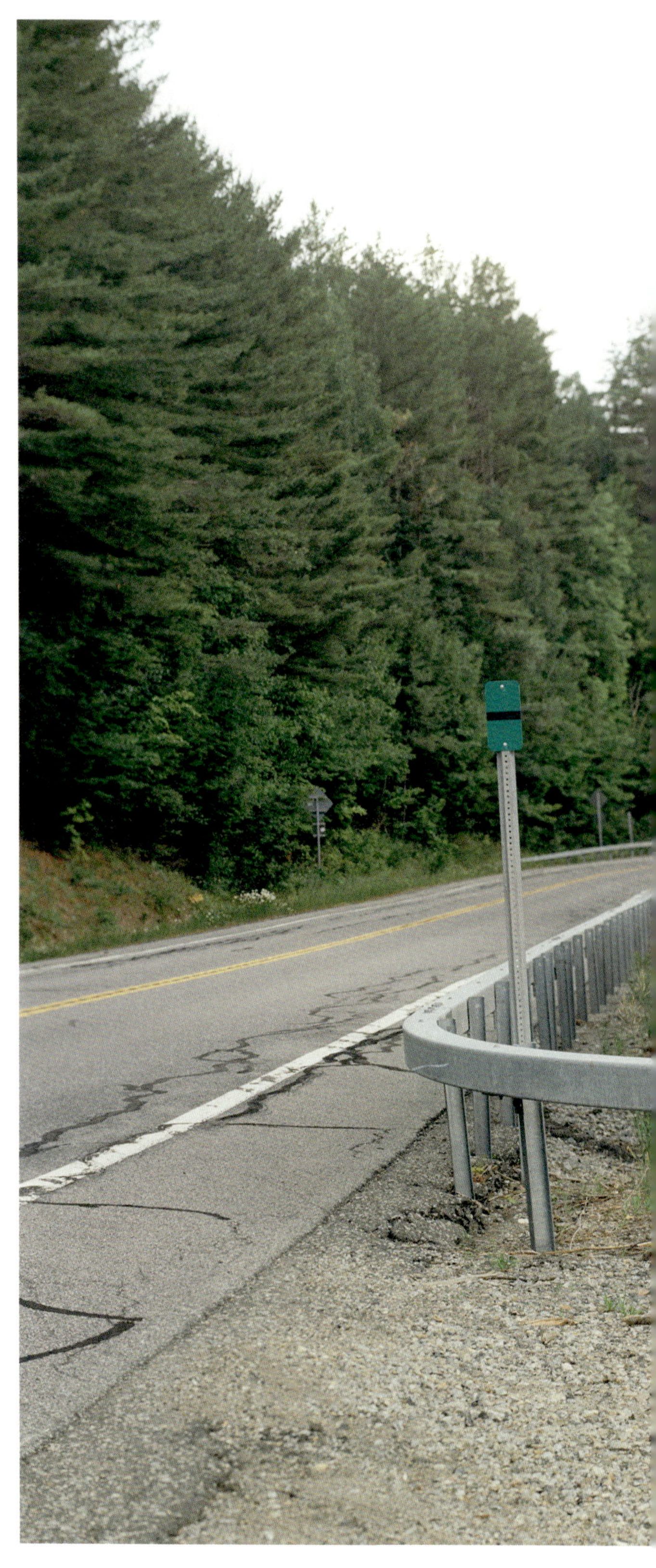

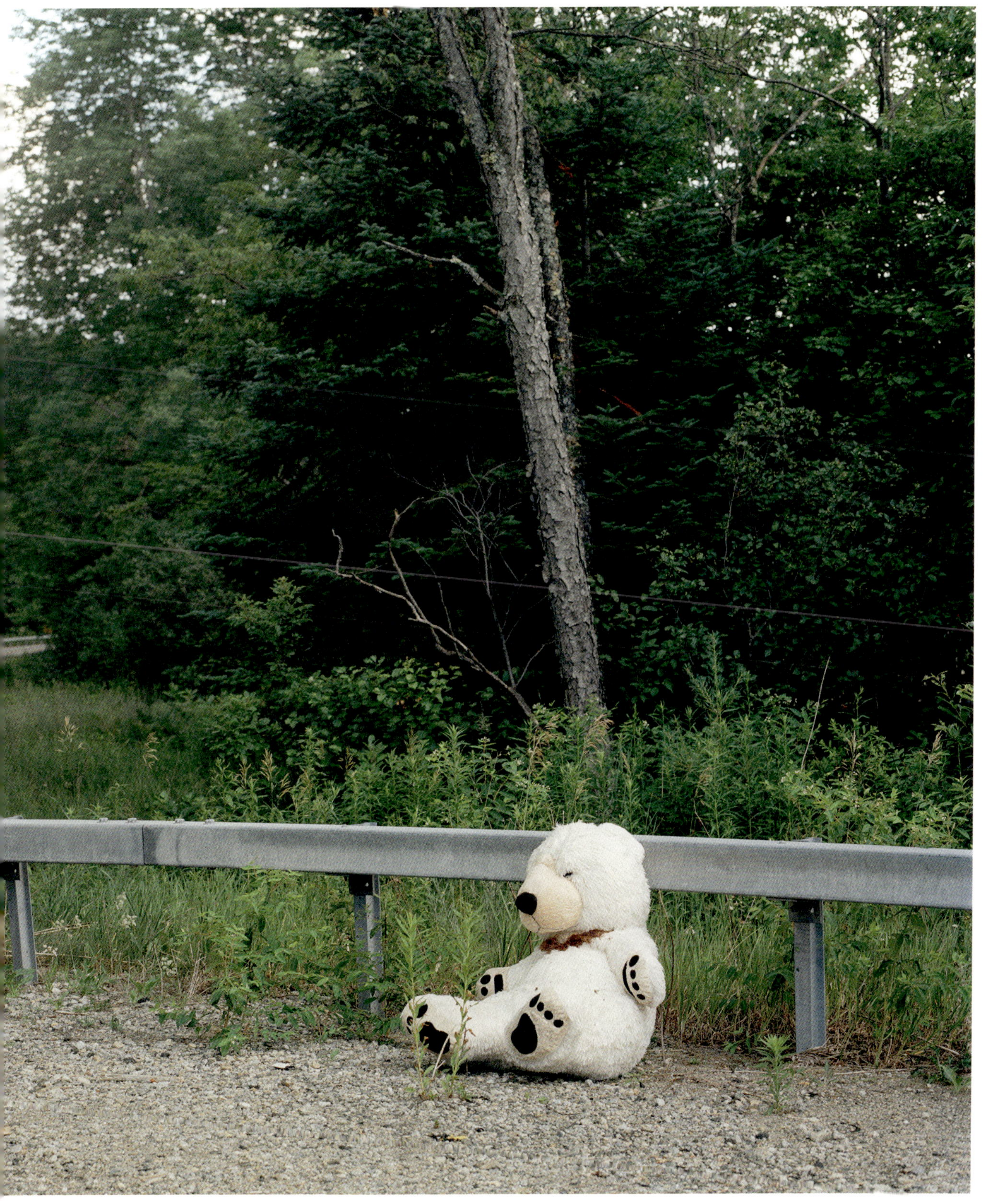

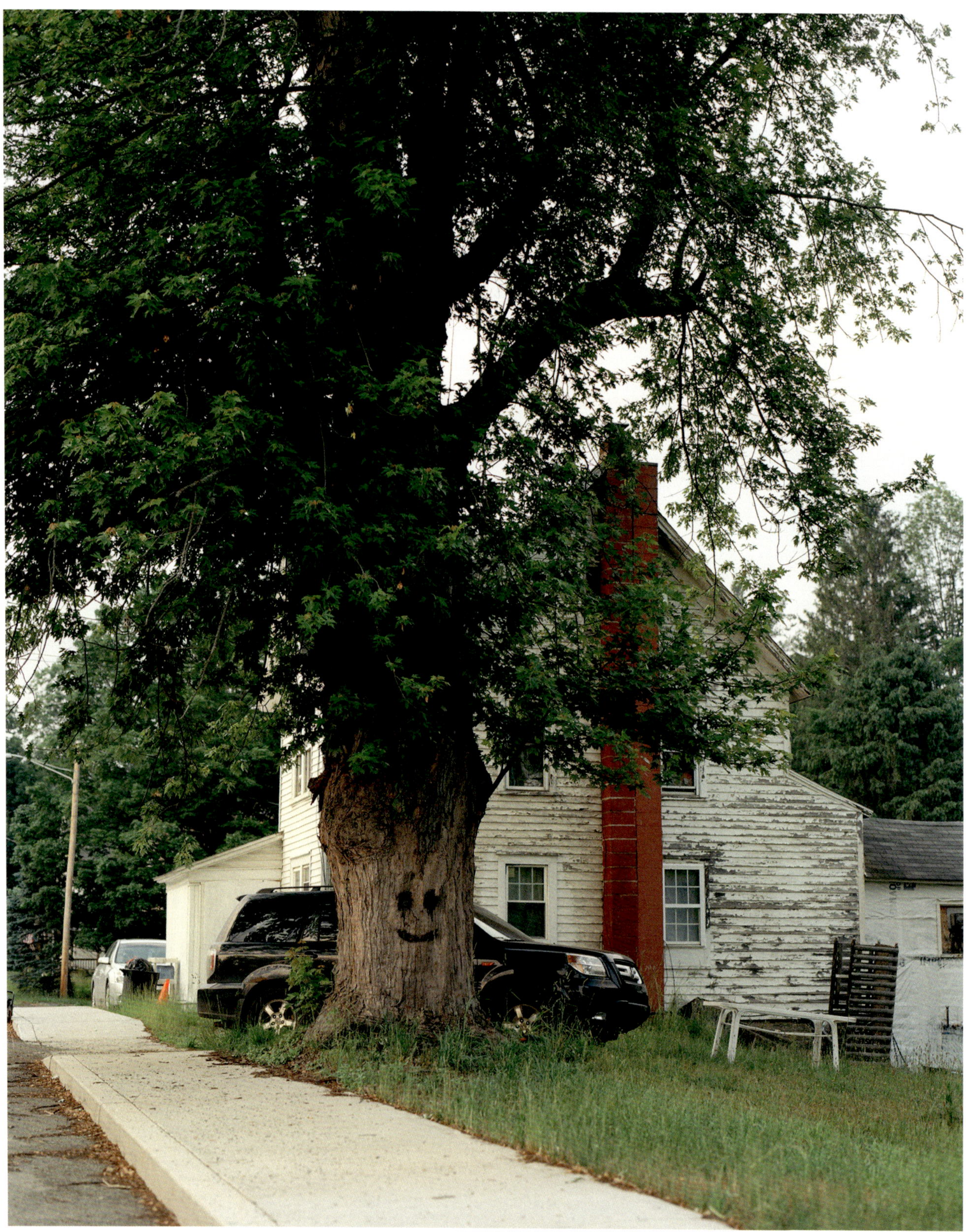

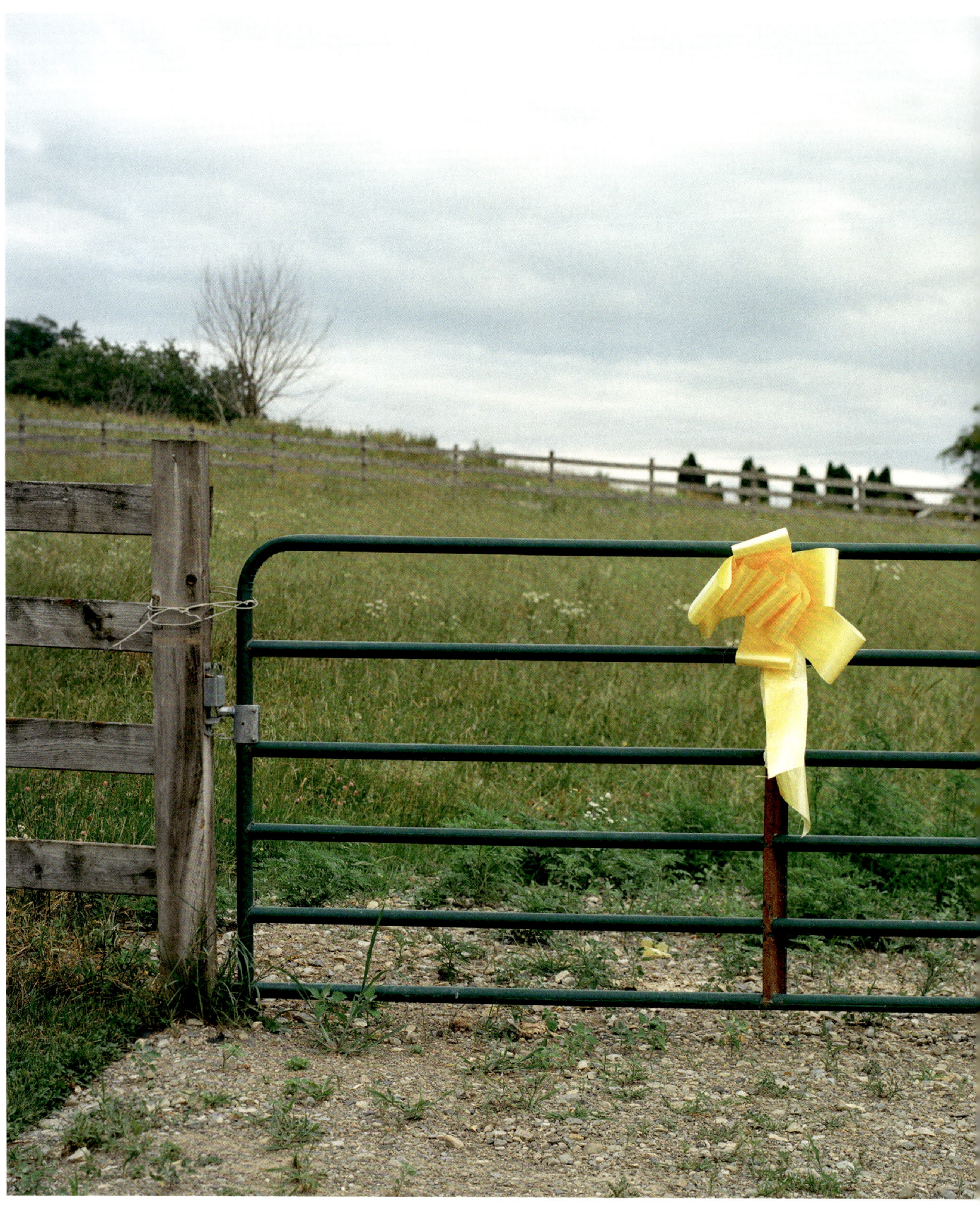

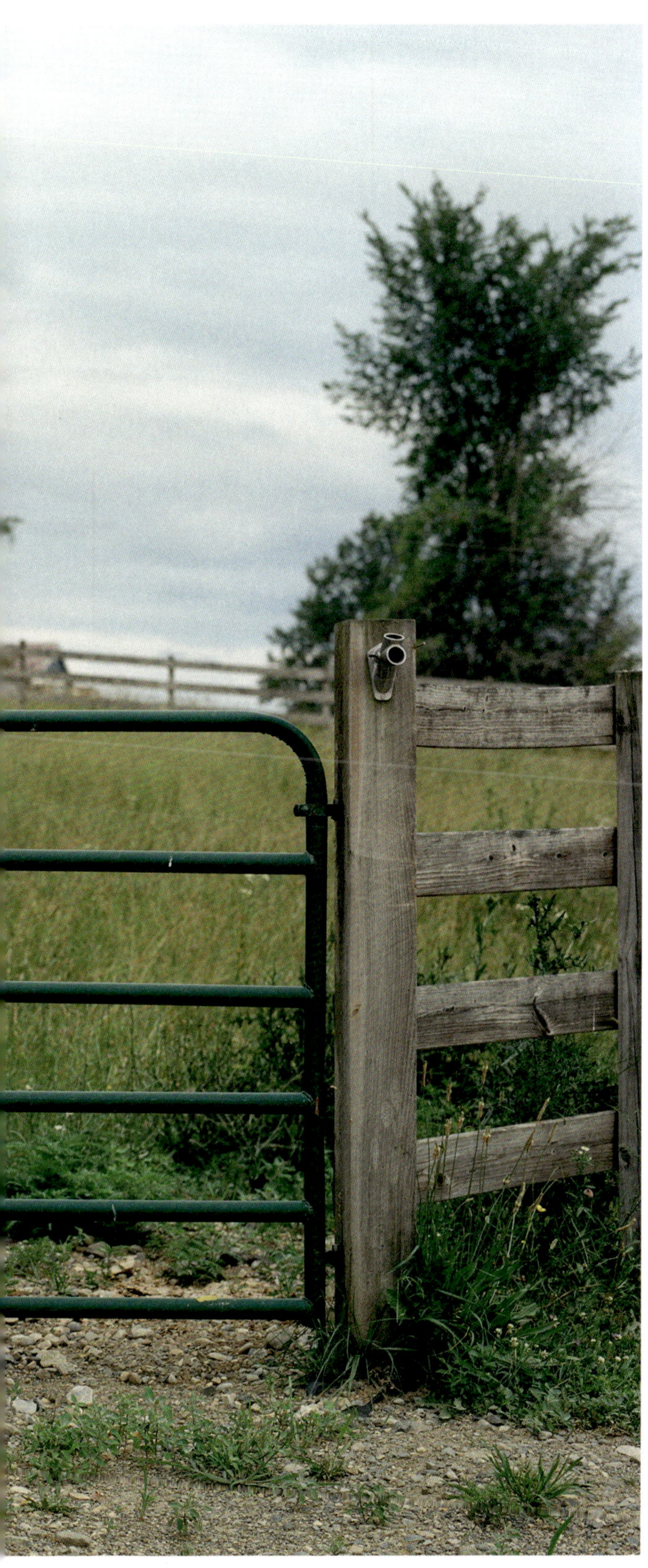

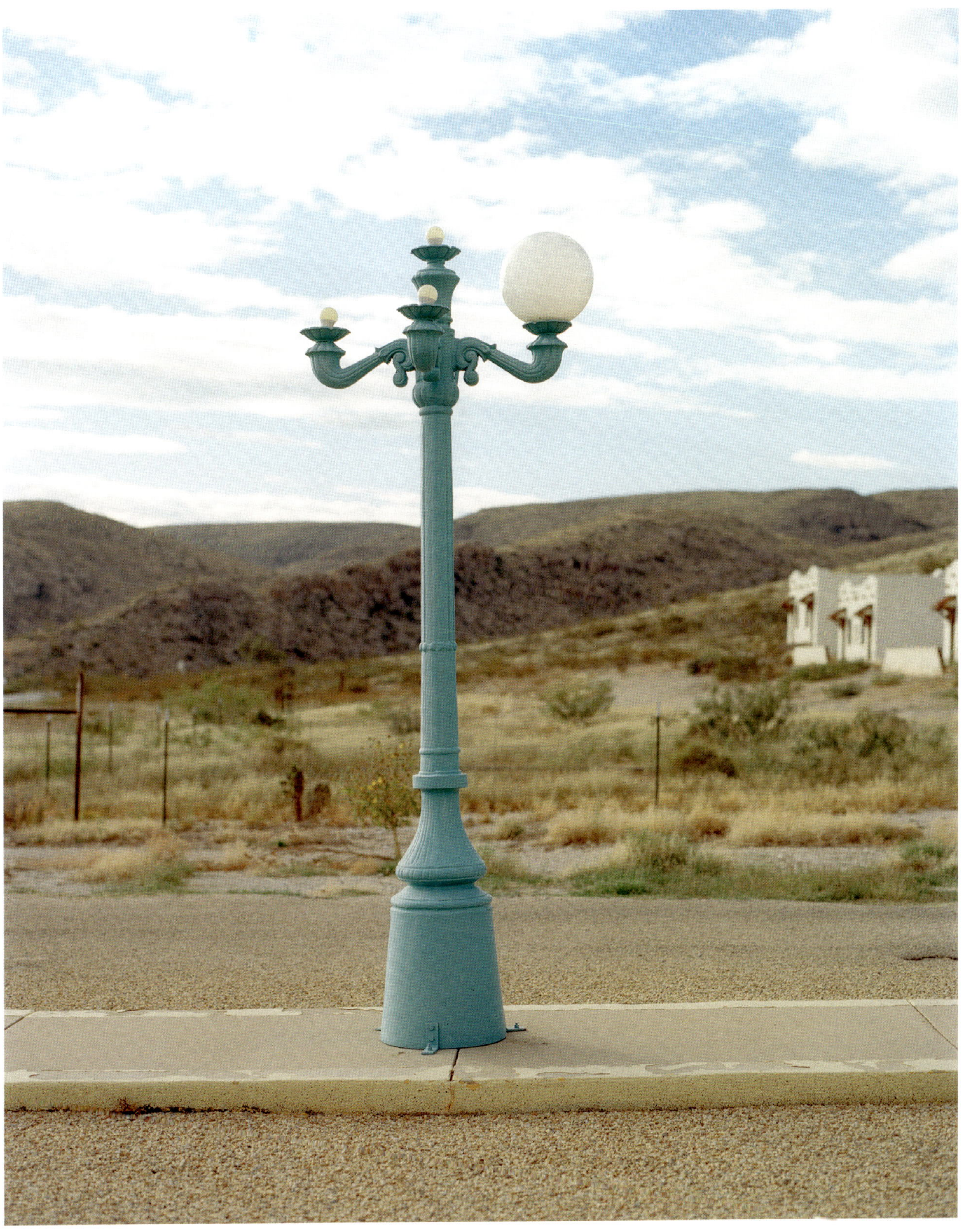

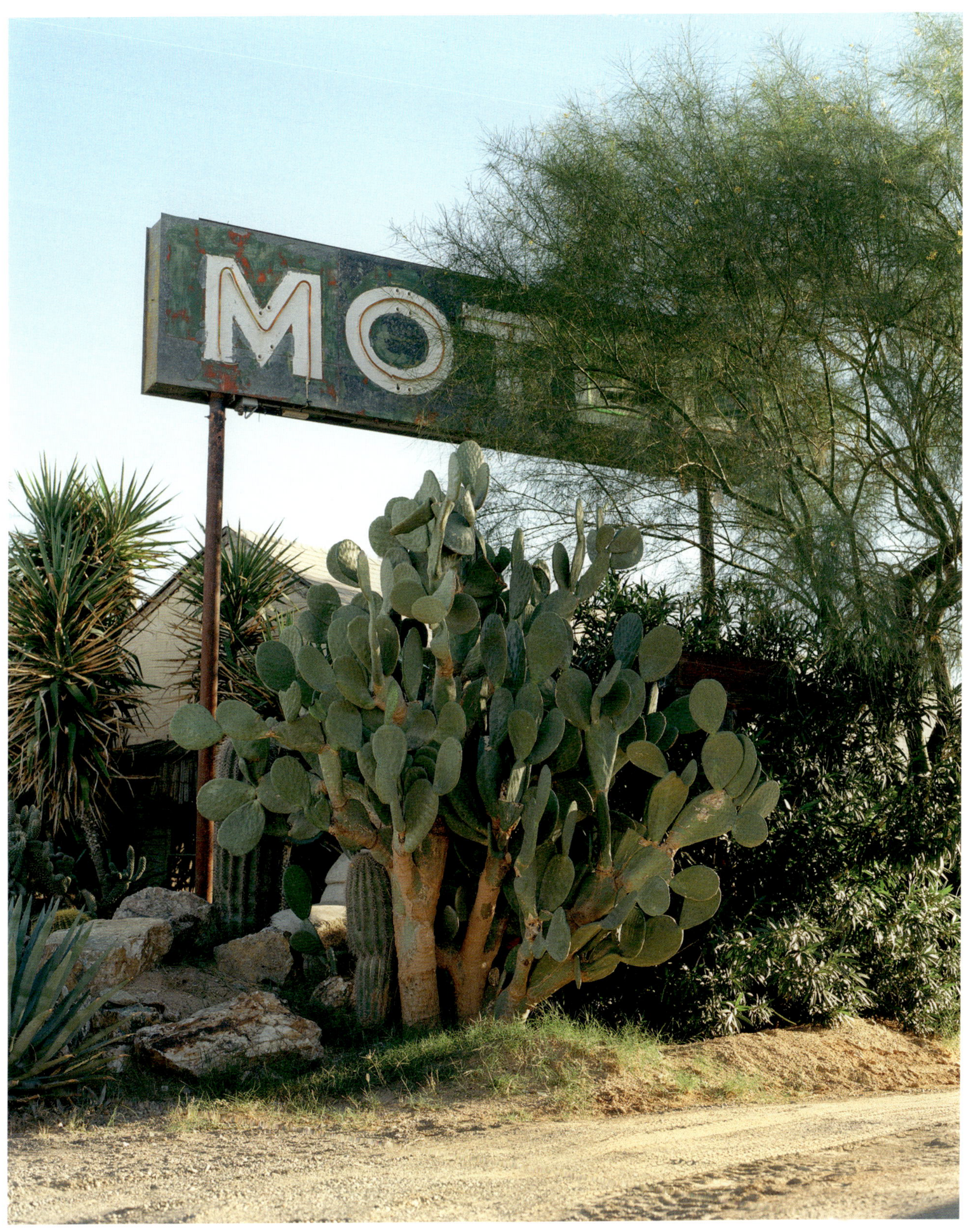
MO

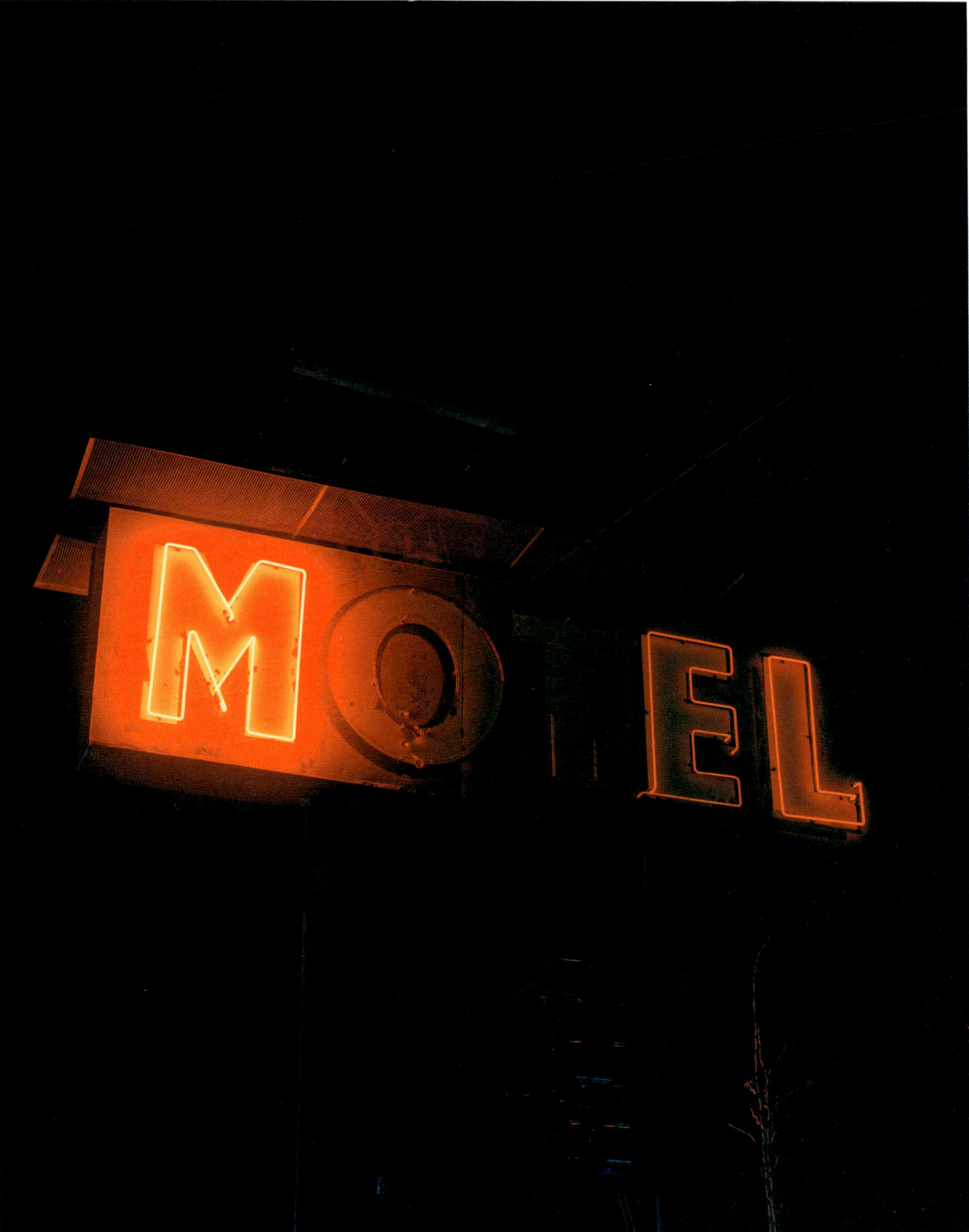
MO EL

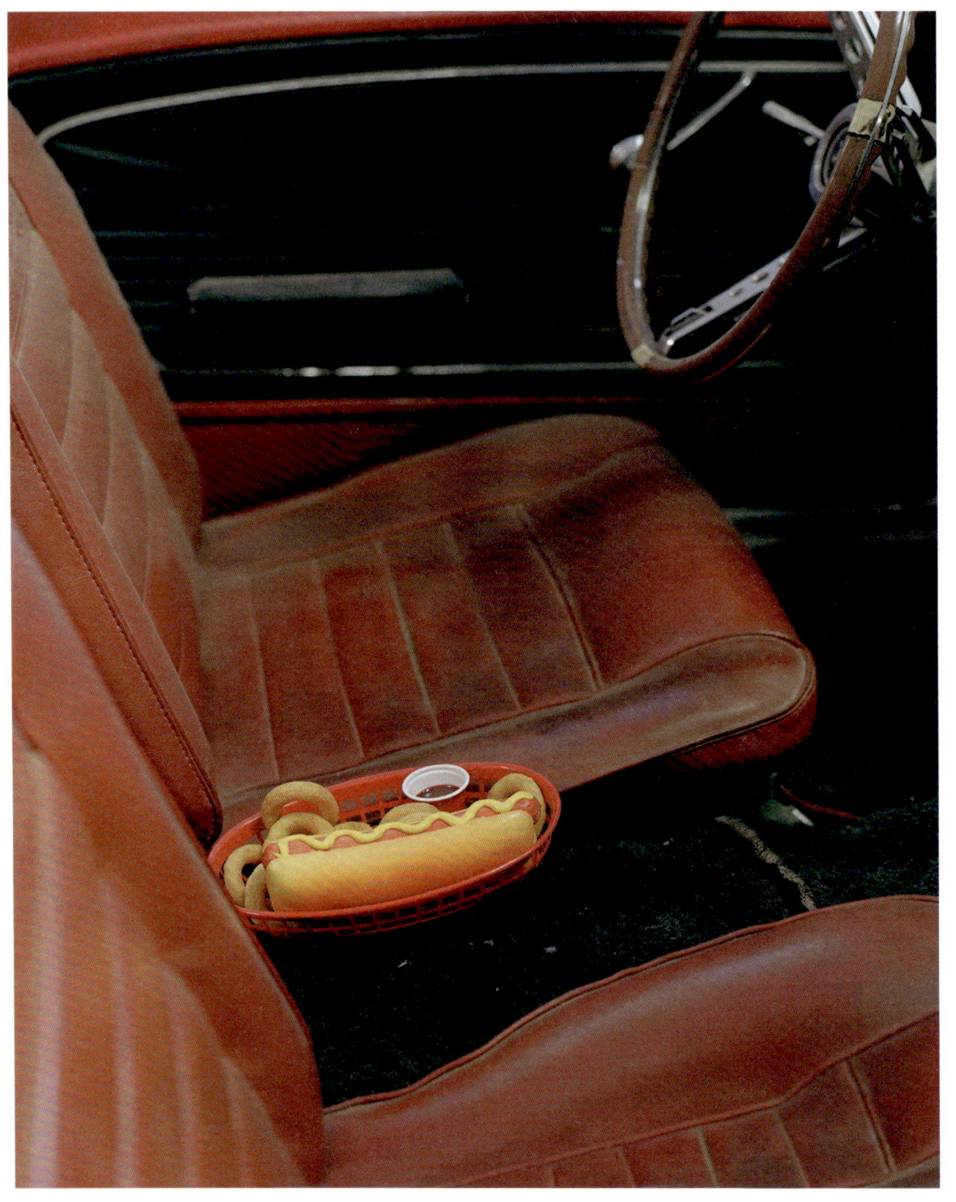

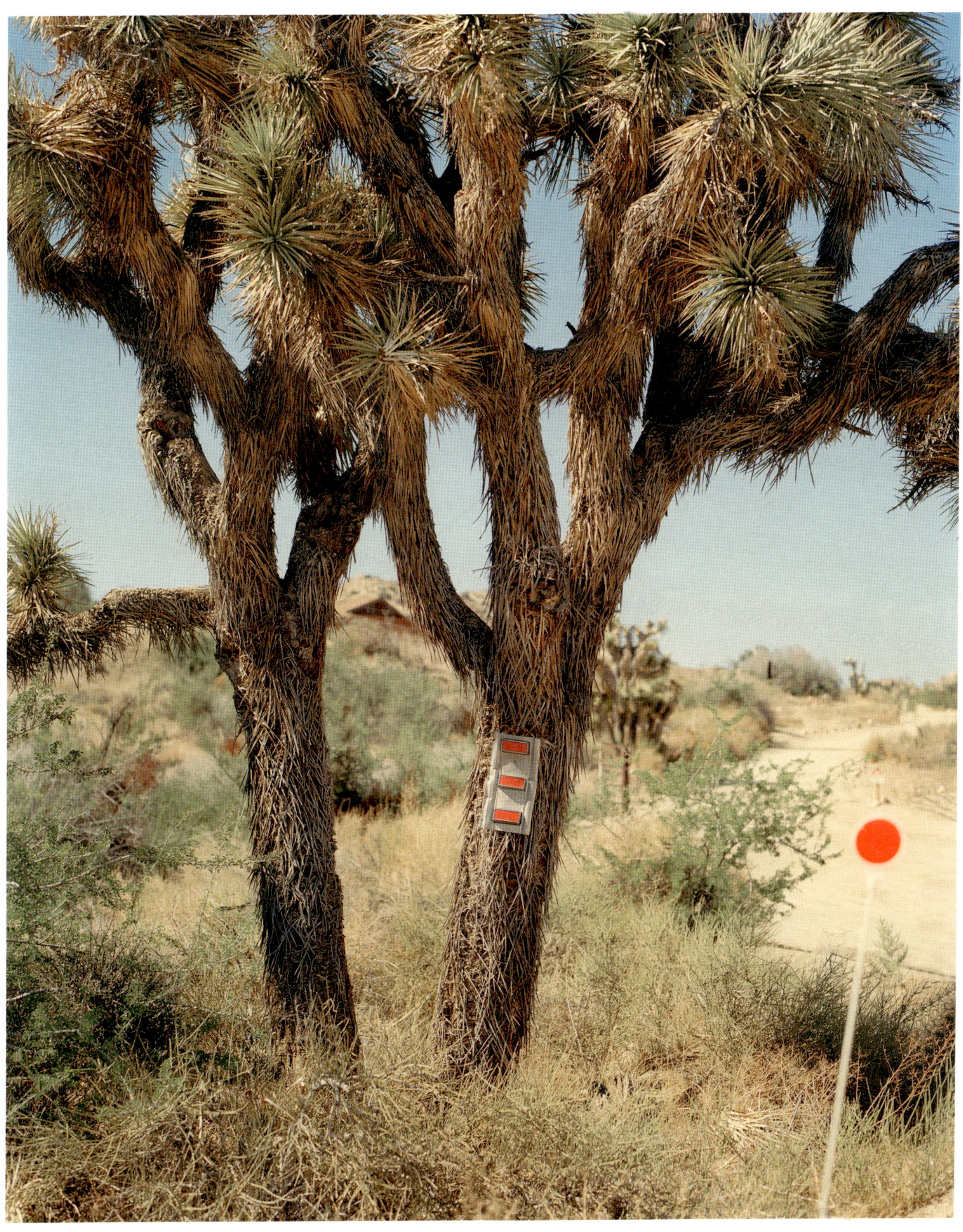

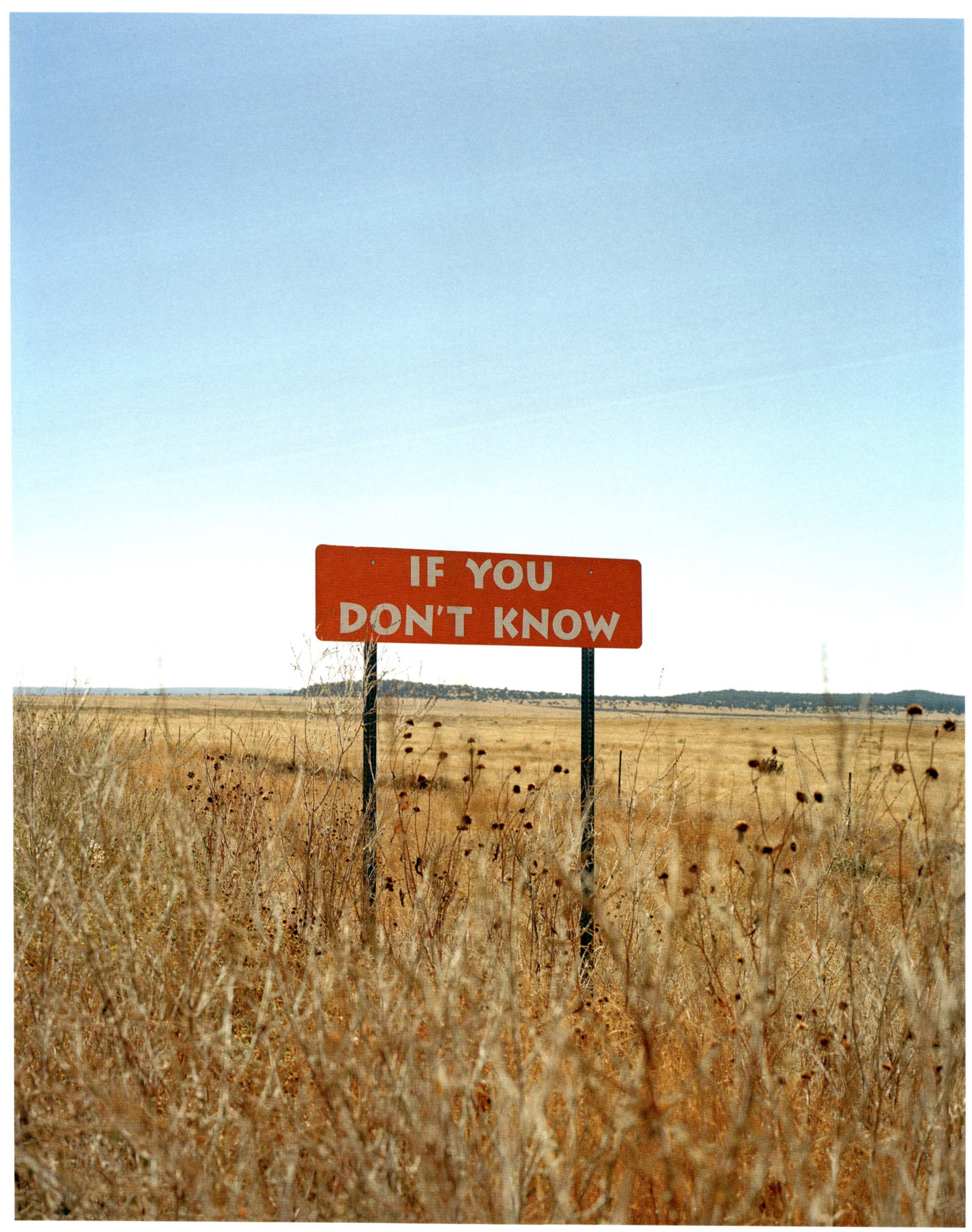
IF YOU
DON'T KNOW

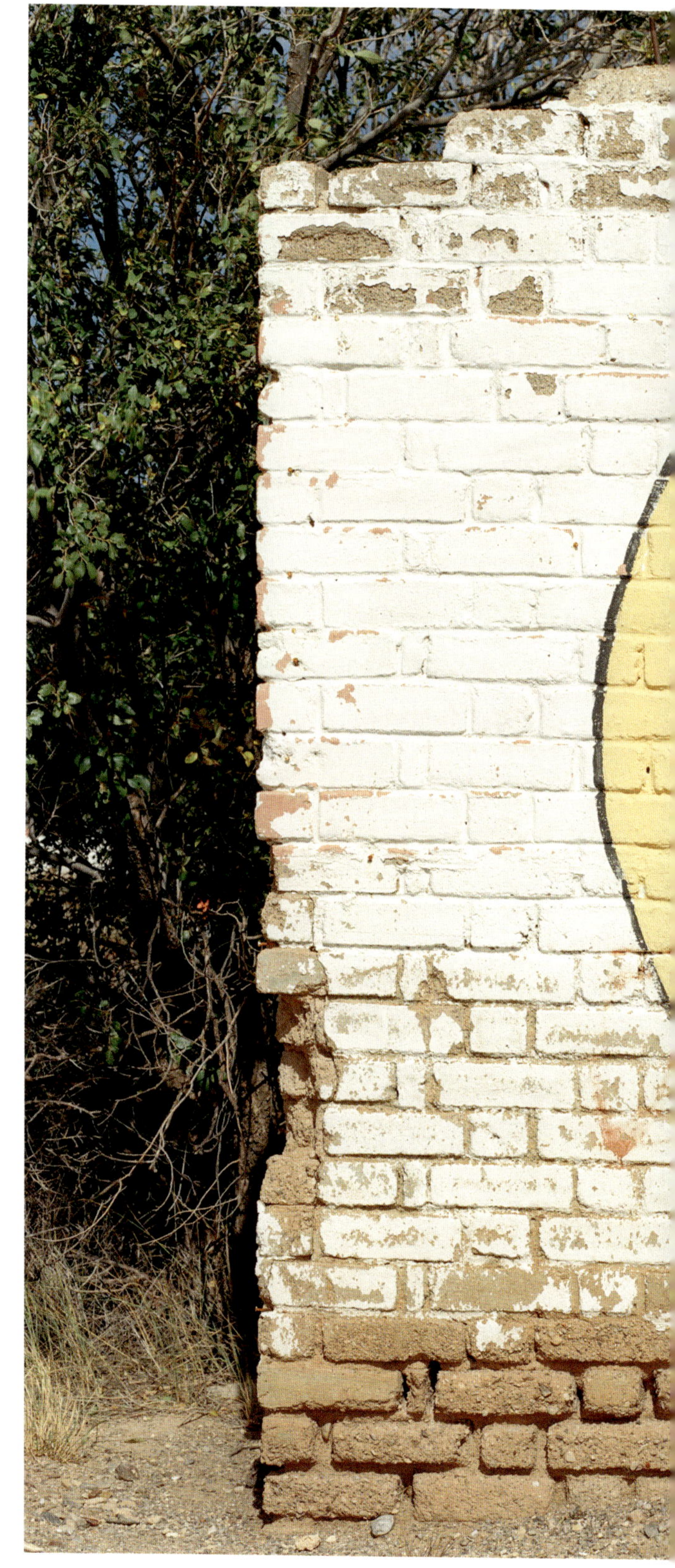

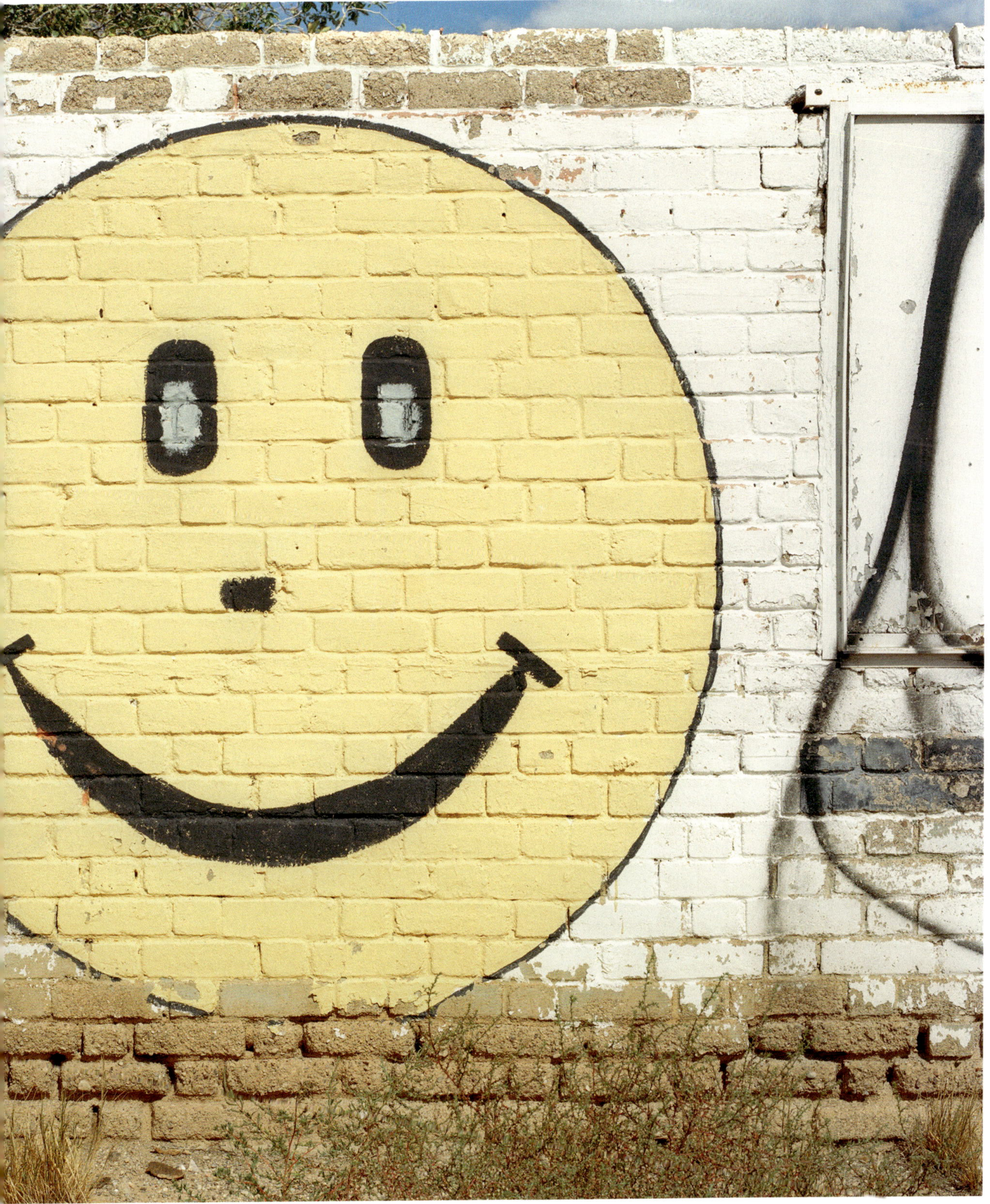

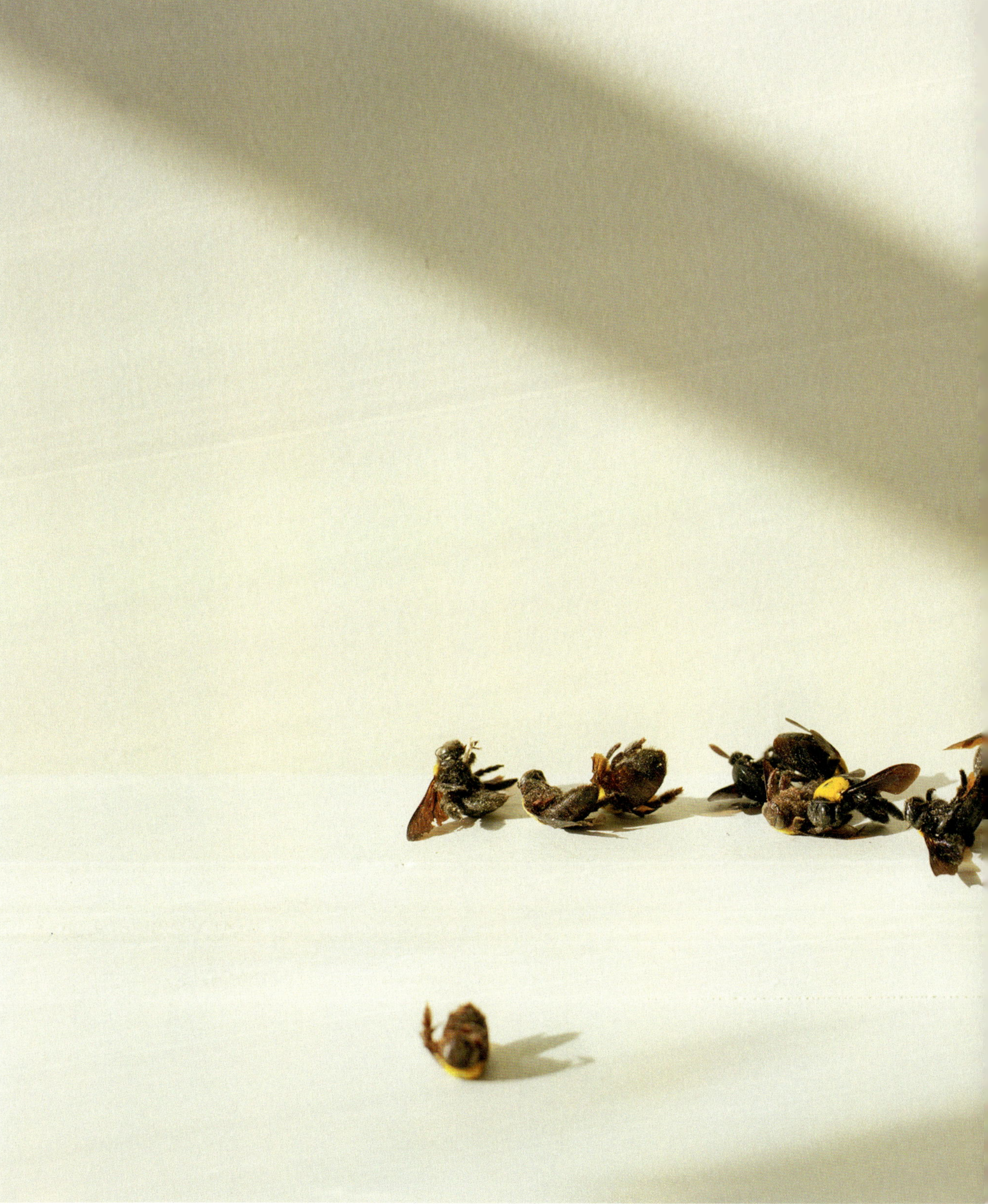

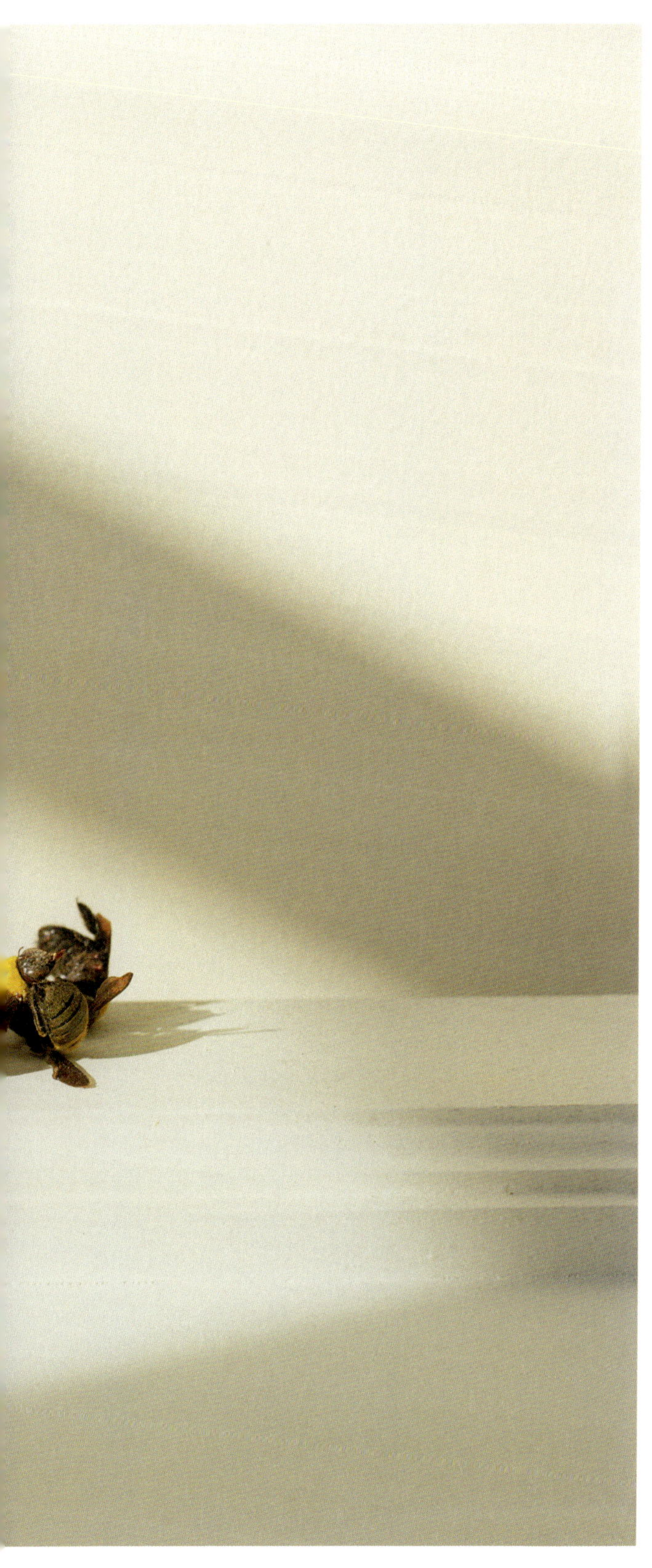

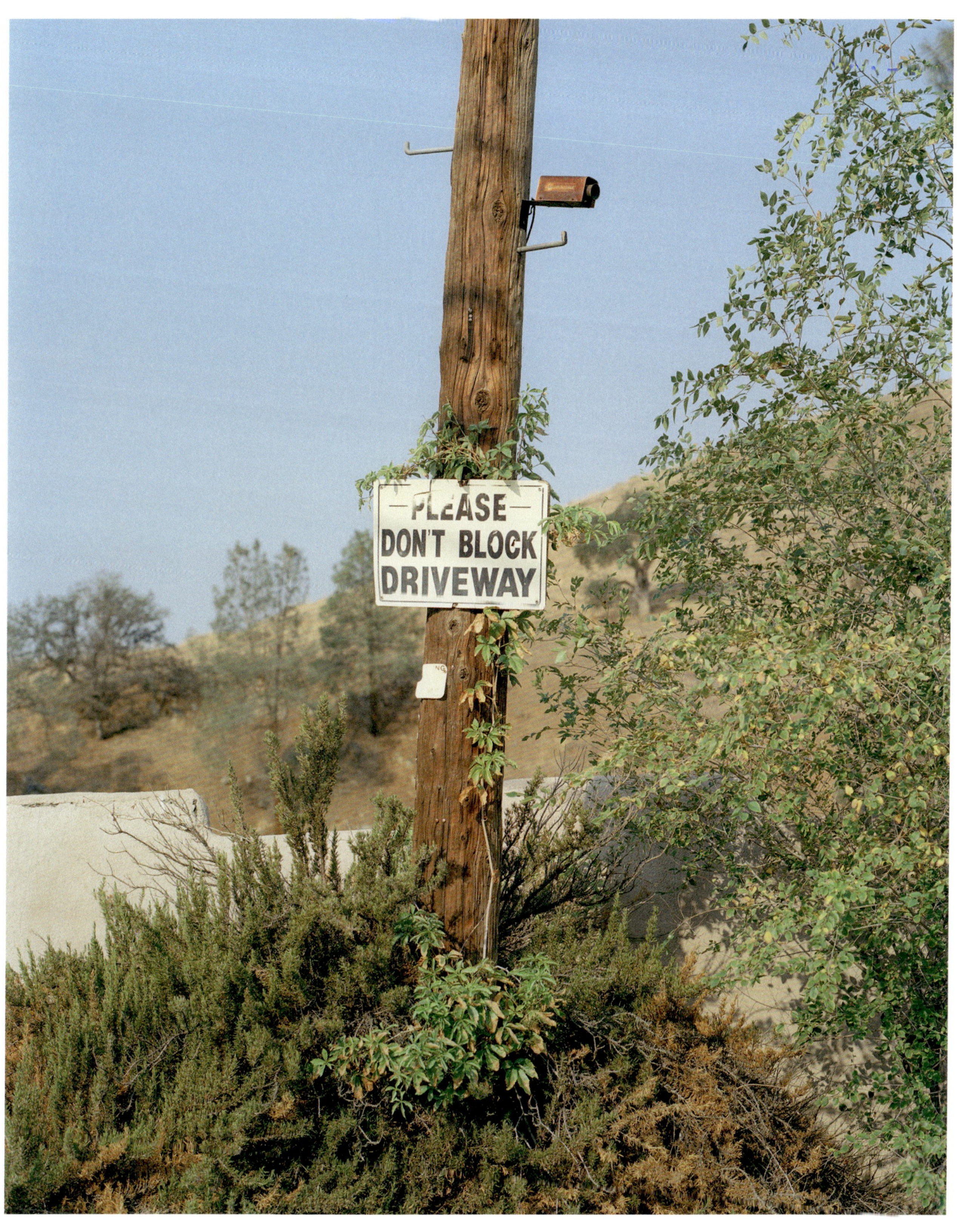
PLEASE
DON'T BLOCK
DRIVEWAY

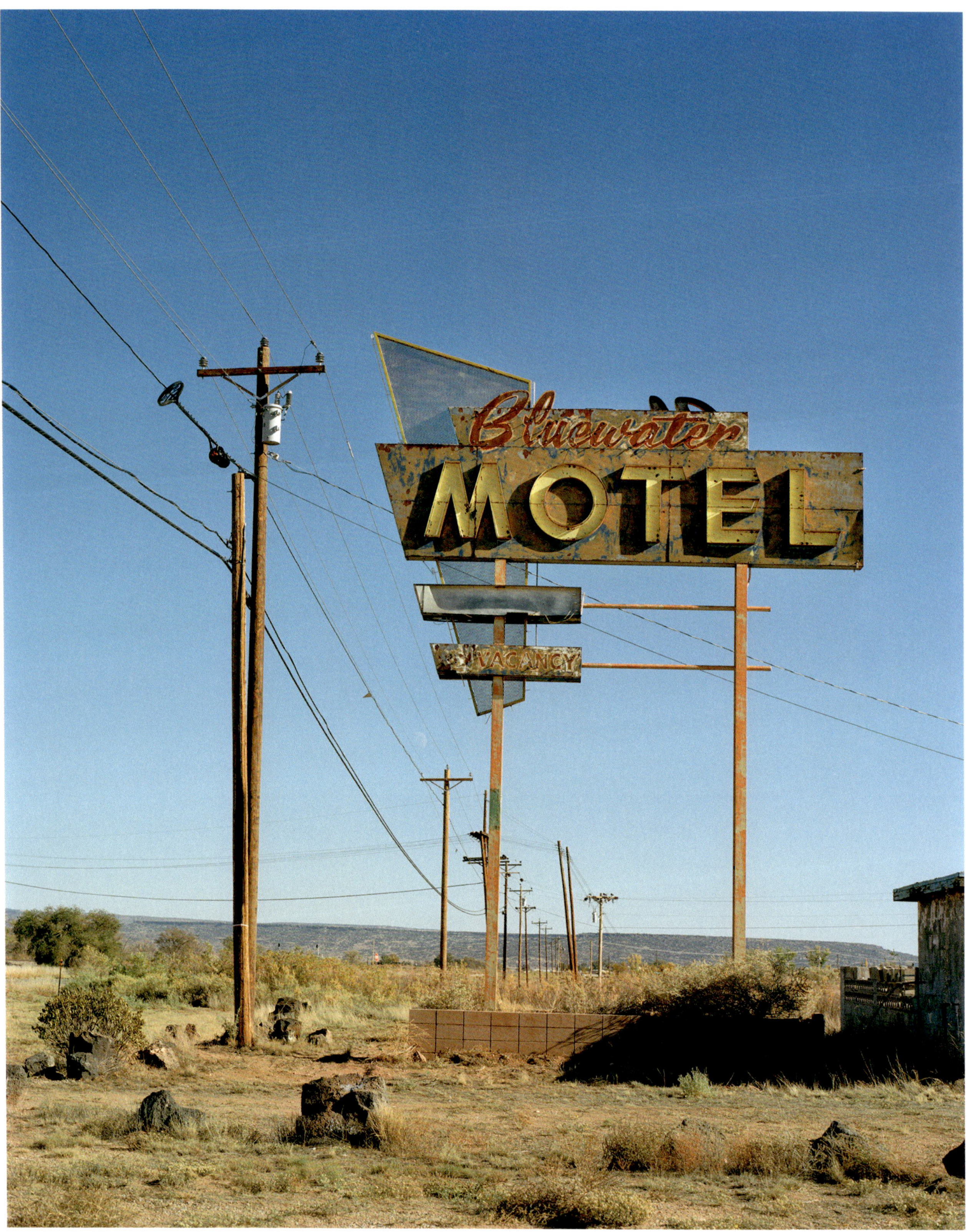
Bluewater
MOTEL
VACANCY

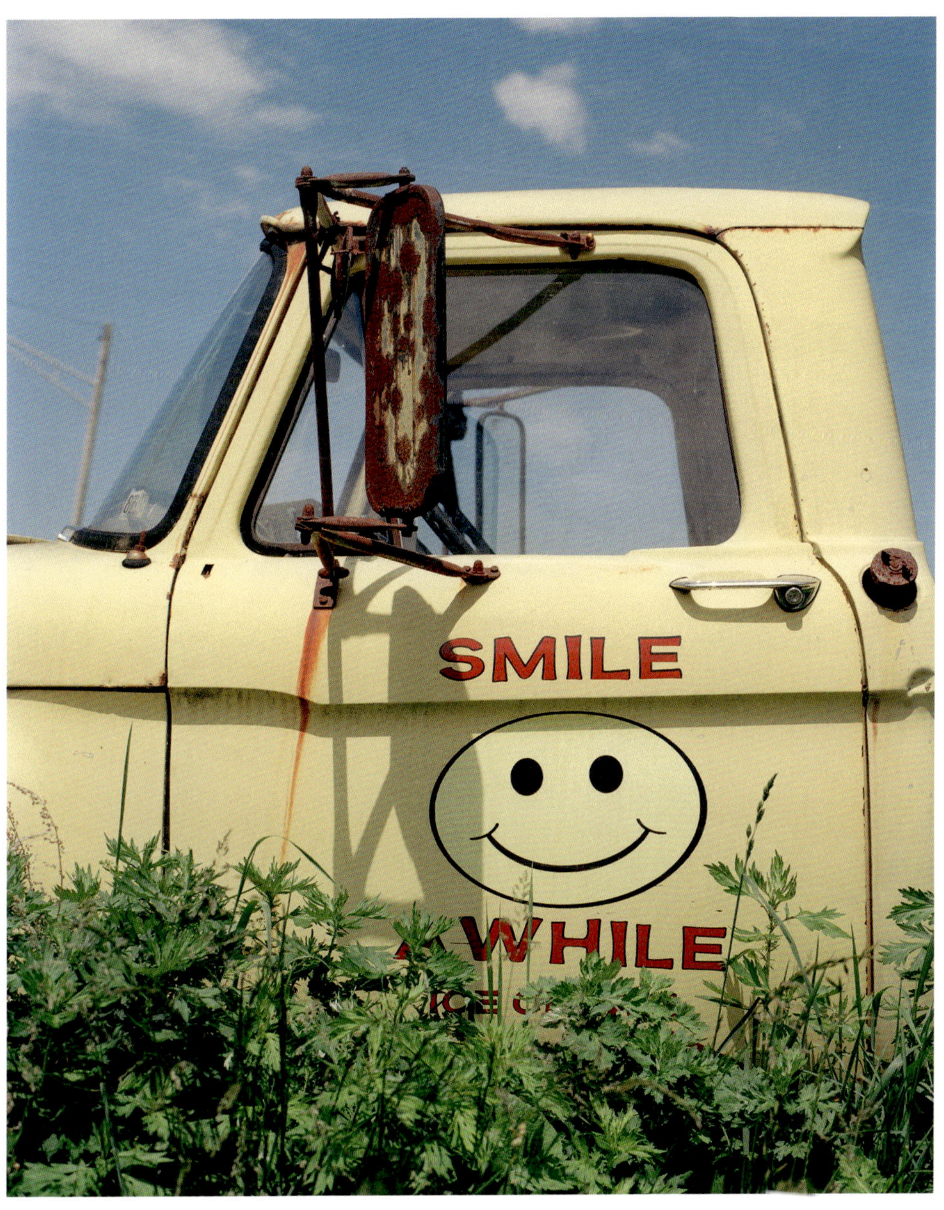
SMILE
AWHILE

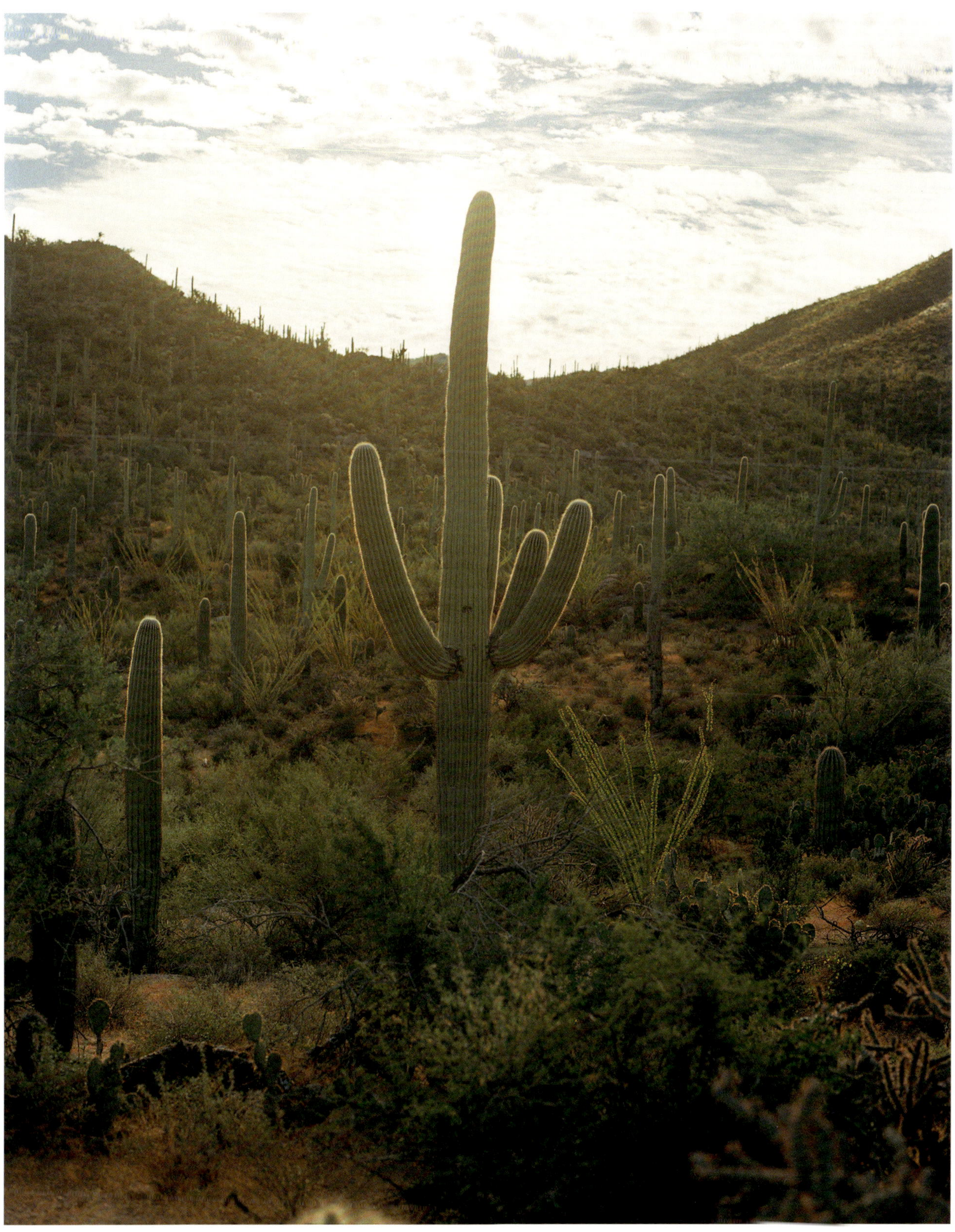

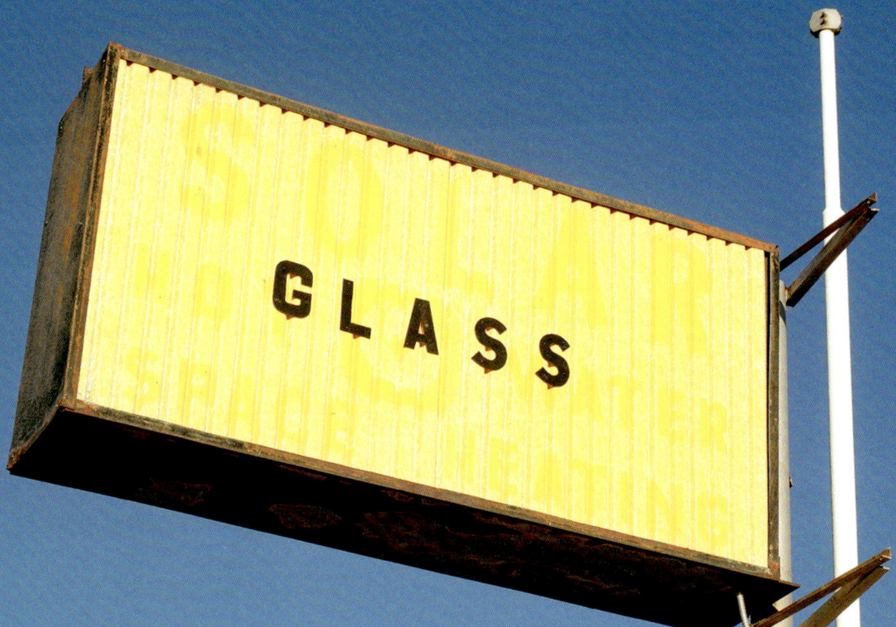
GLASS

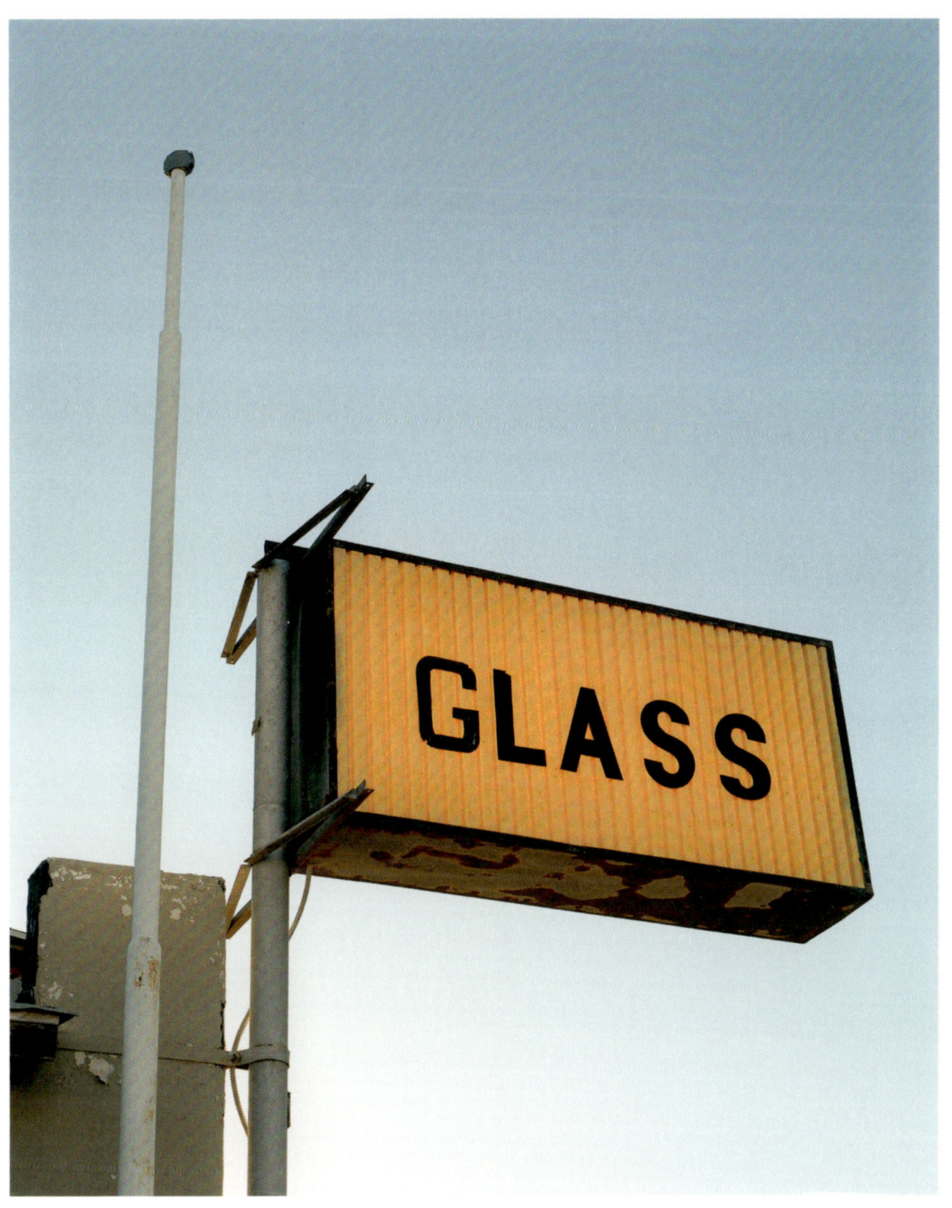
GLASS

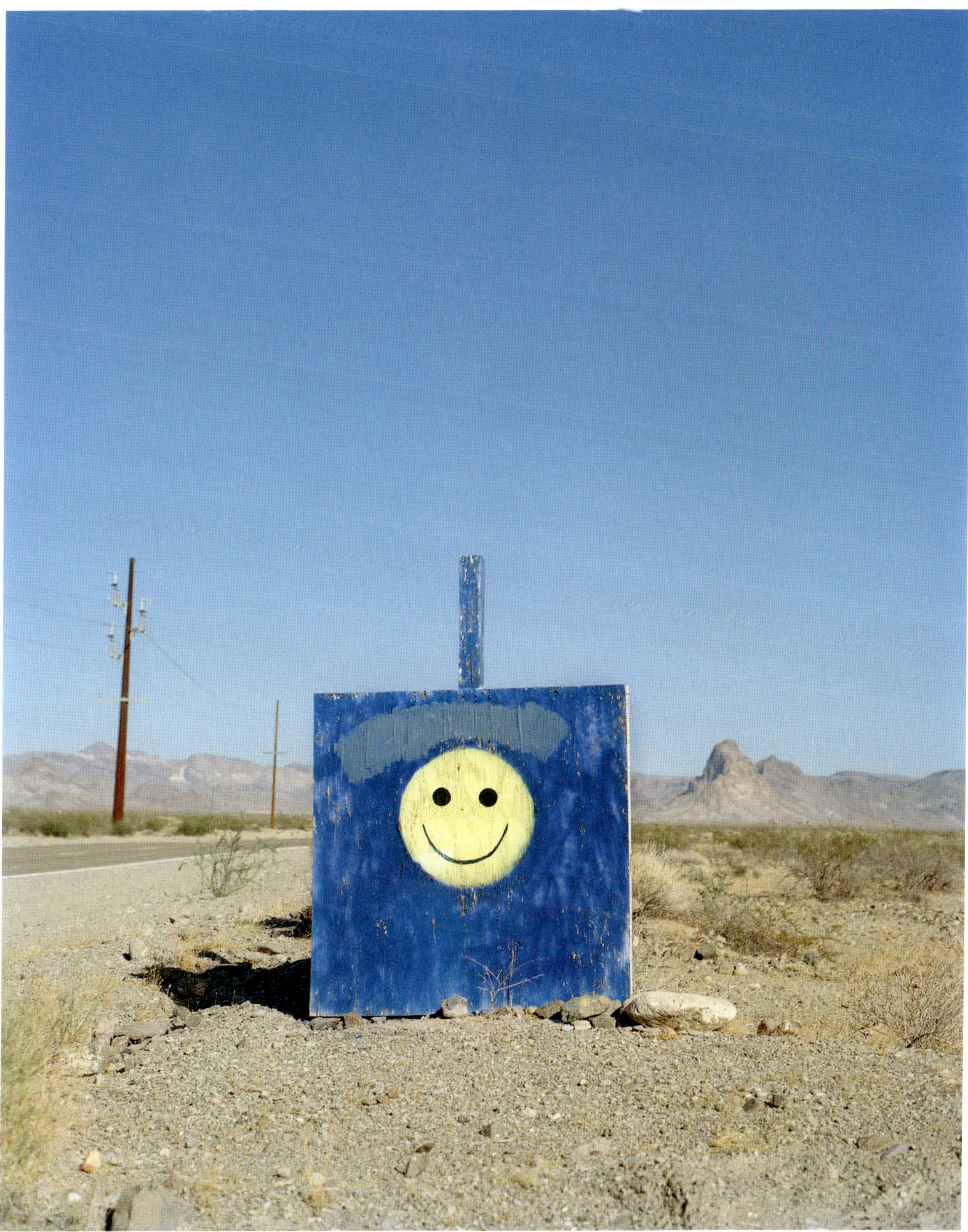

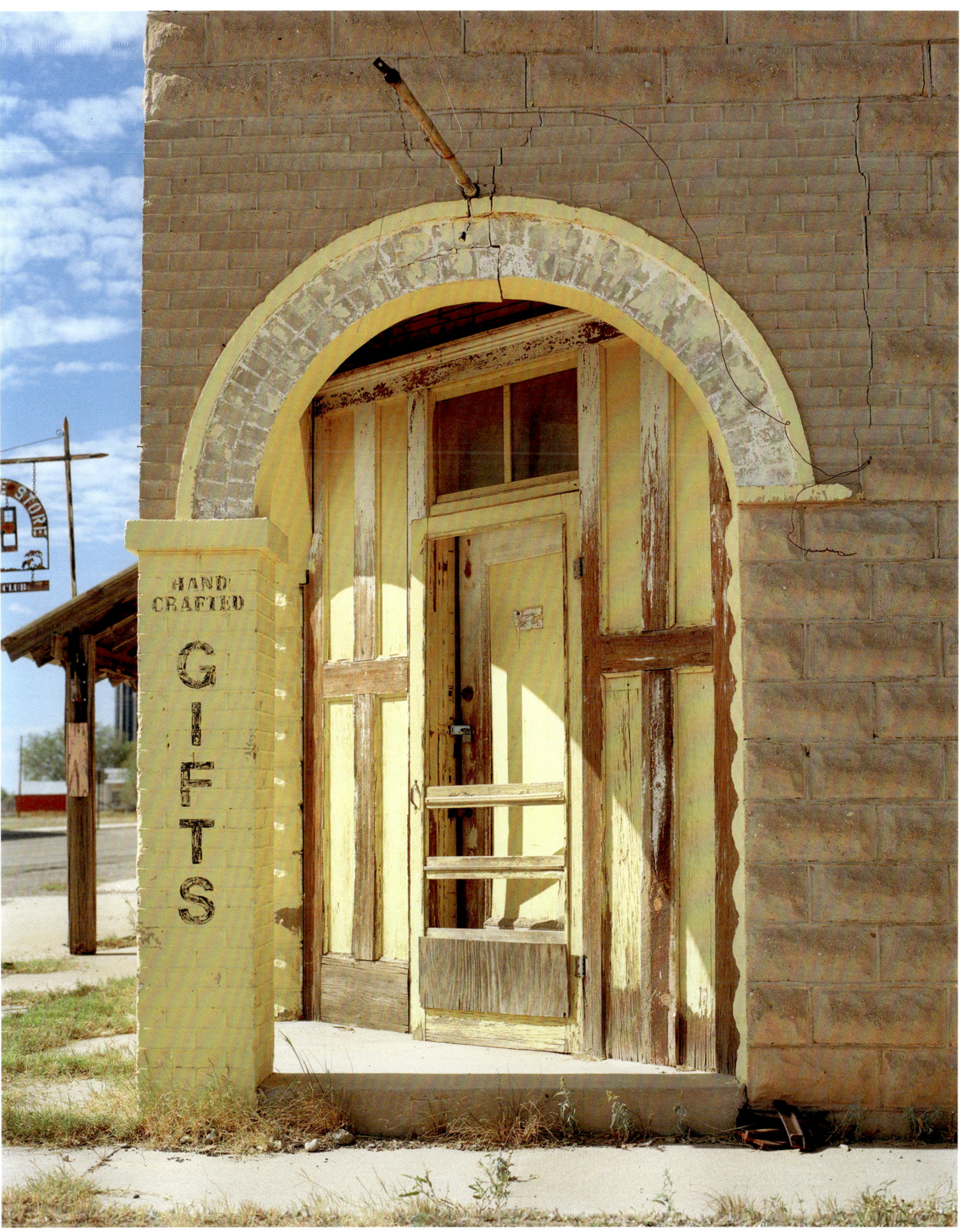
STORE
CLUB
HAND
CRAFTED
GIFTS

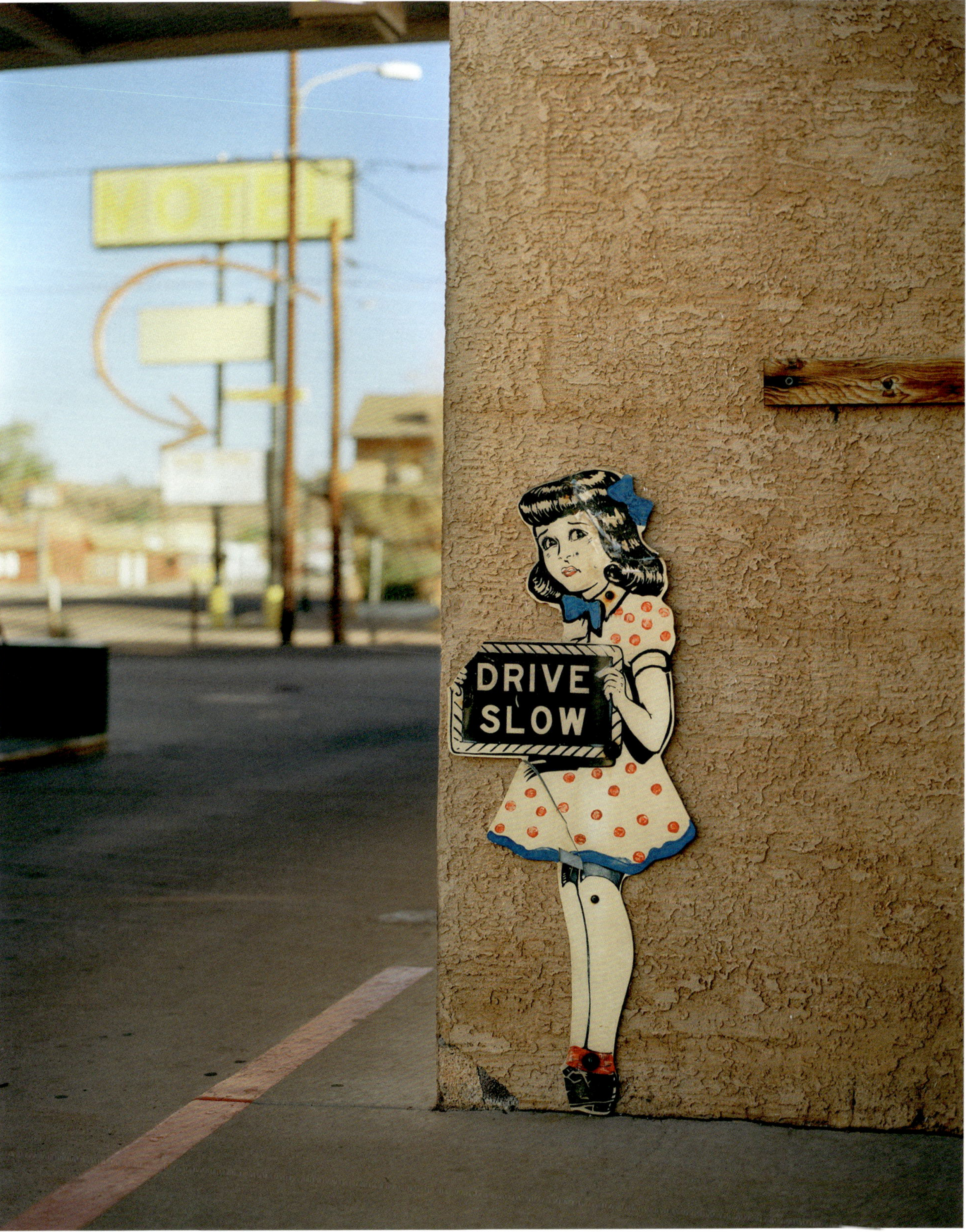
DRIVE
SLOW

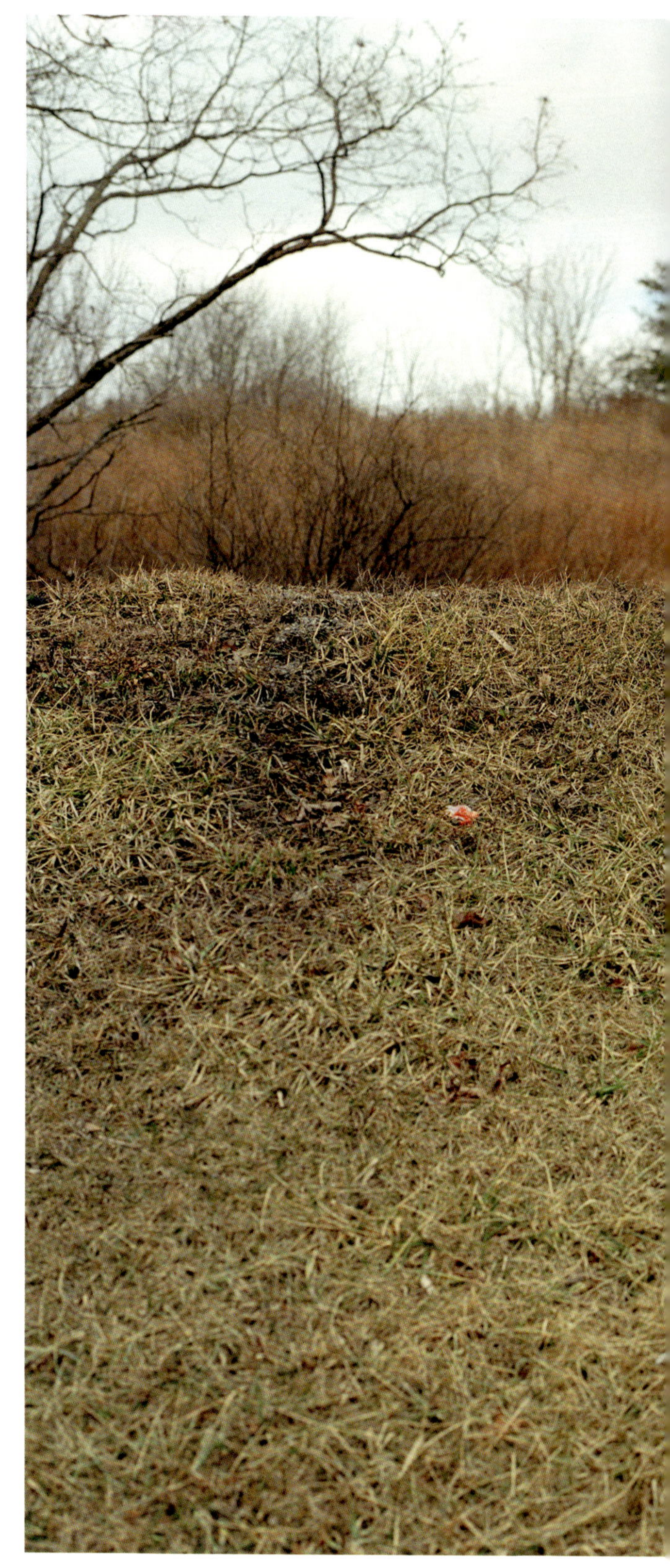

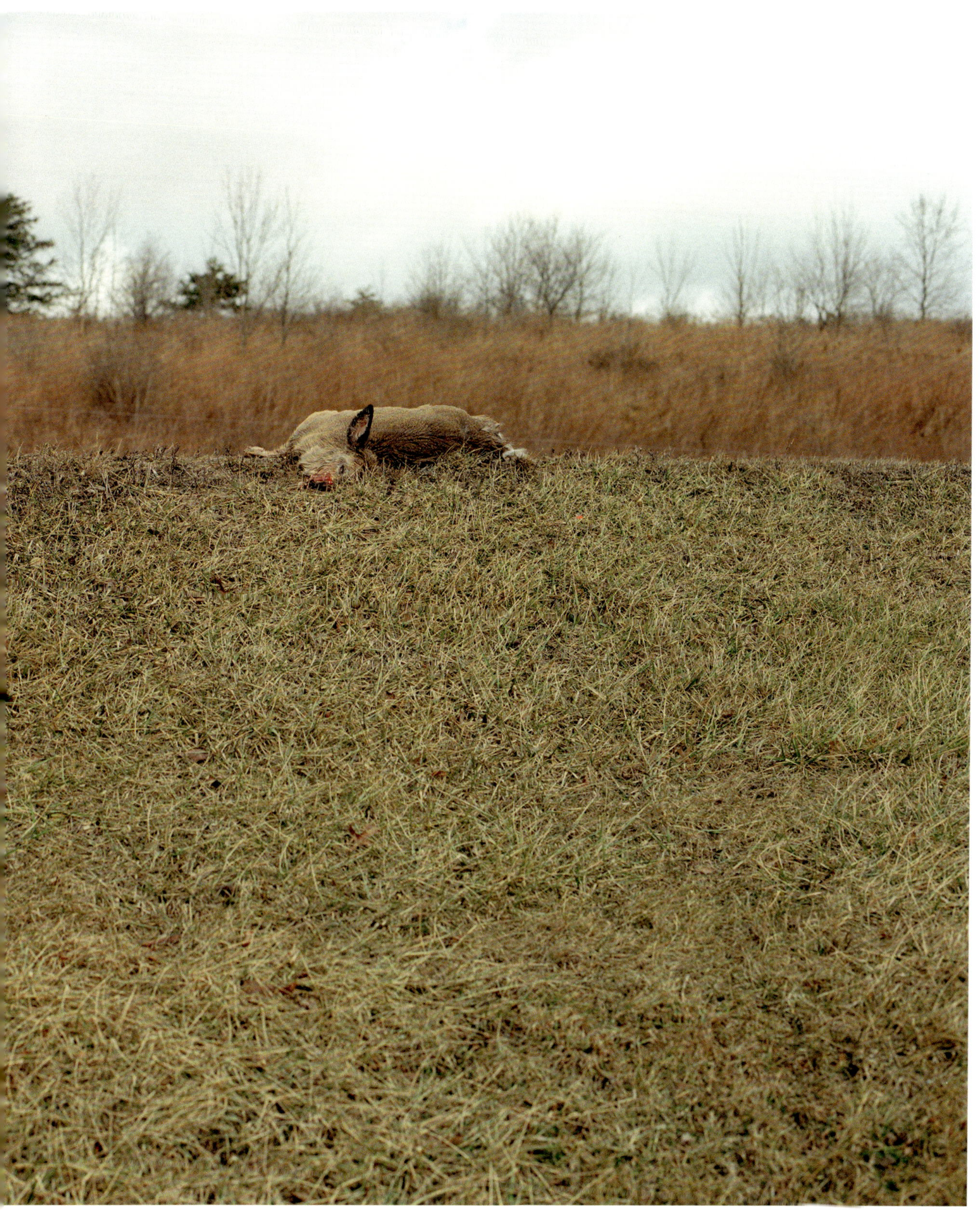

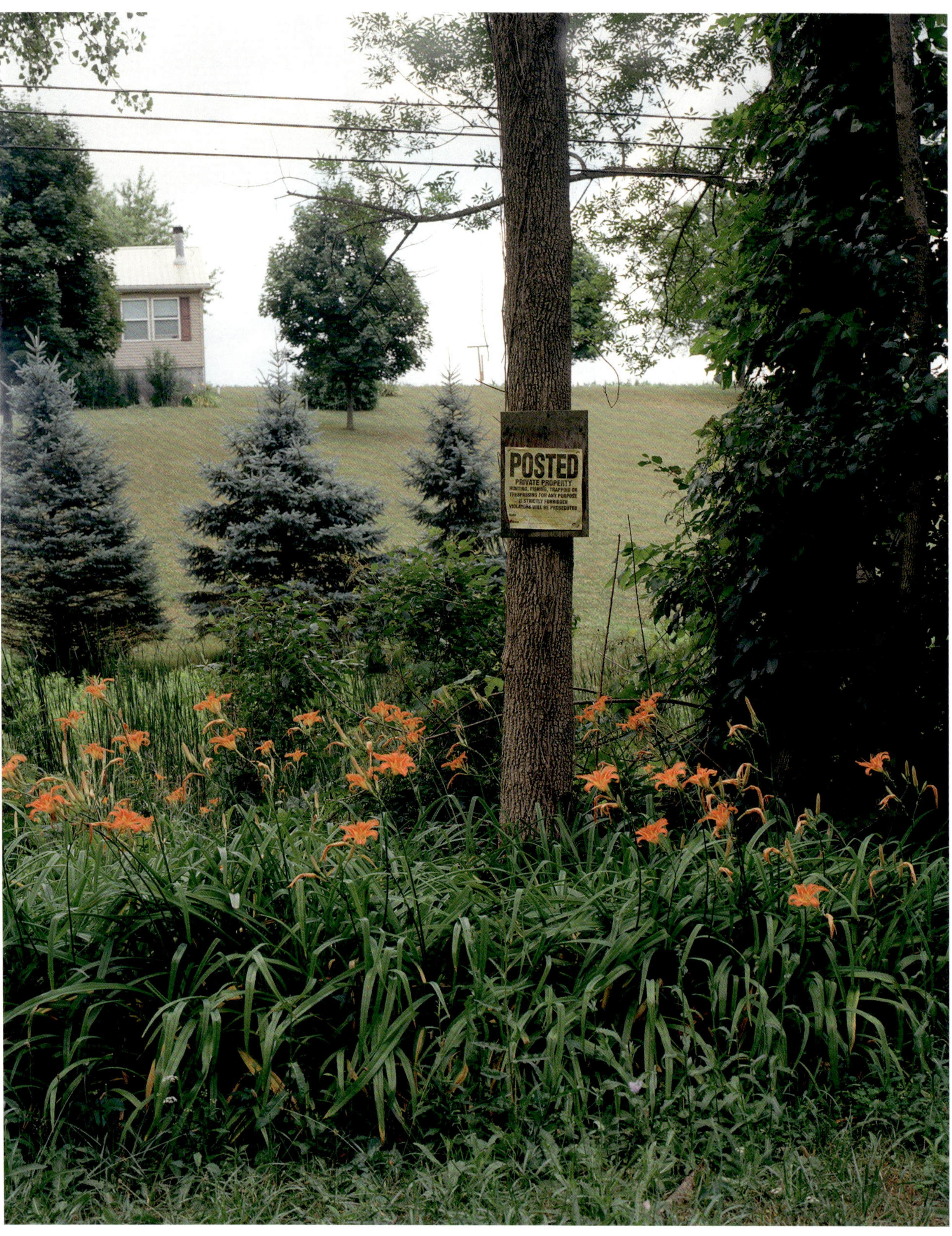
POSTED
PRIVATE PROPERTY
HUNTING, FISHING, TRAPPING OR
TRESPASSING FOR ANY PURPOSE
IS STRICTLY FORBIDDEN
VIOLATORS WILL BE PROSECUTED

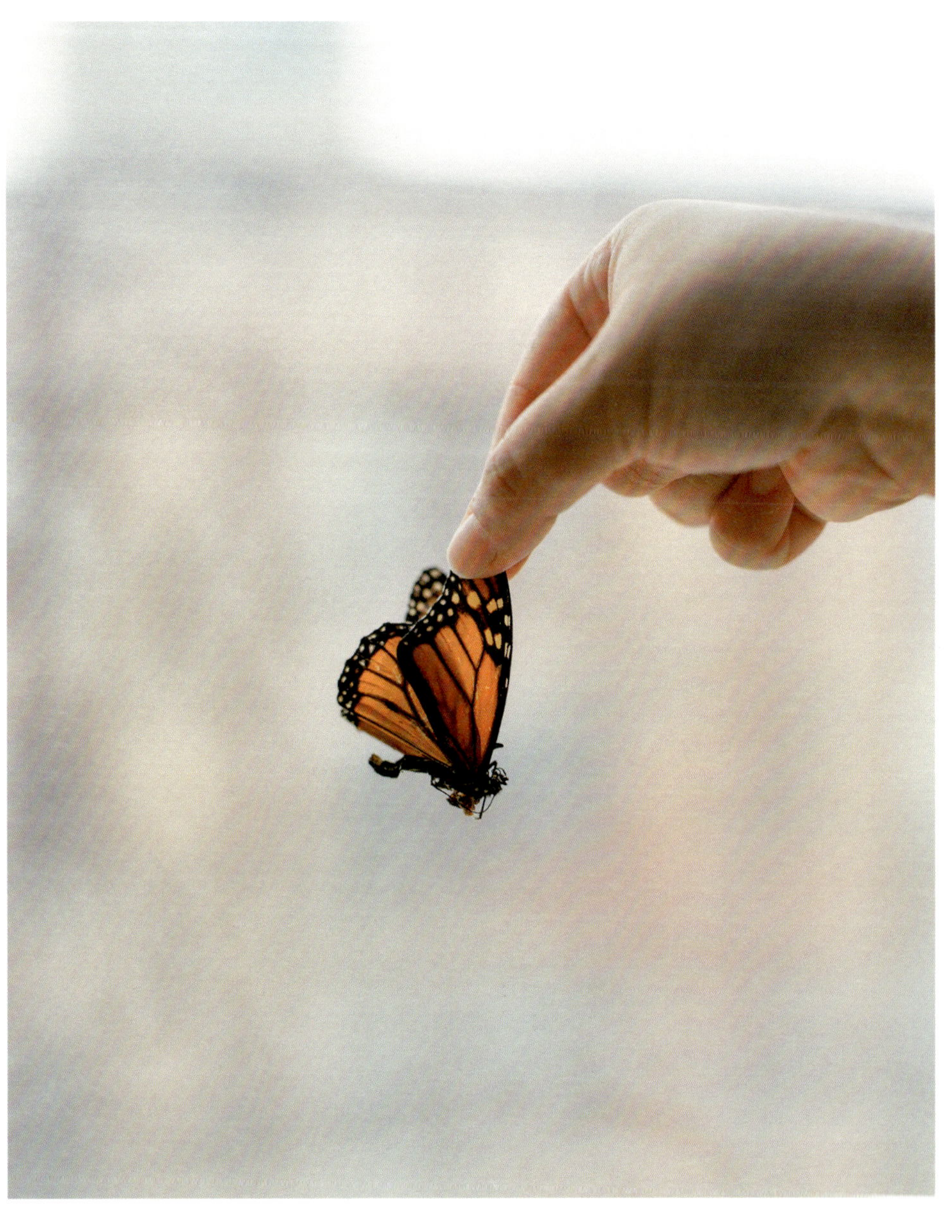

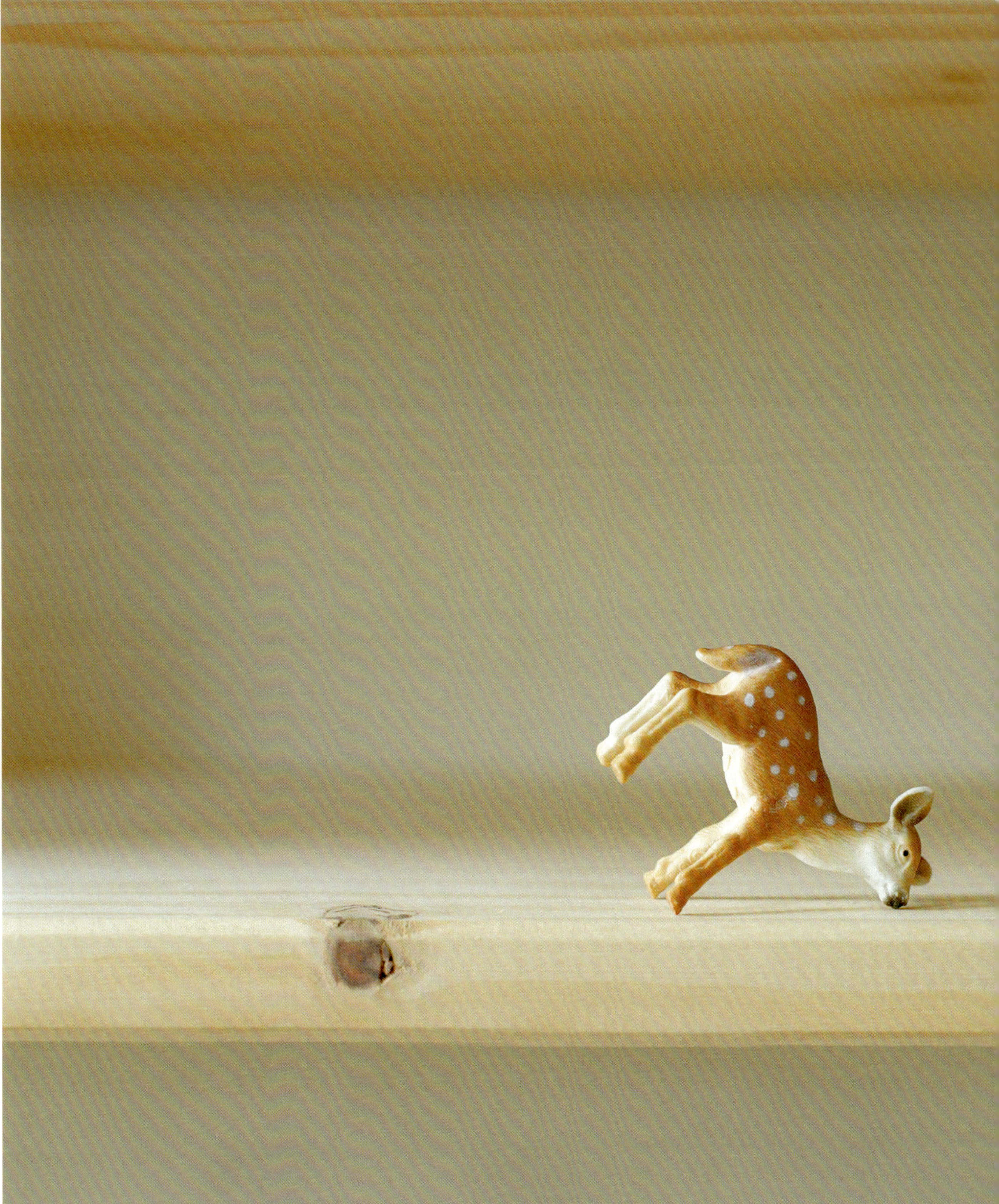

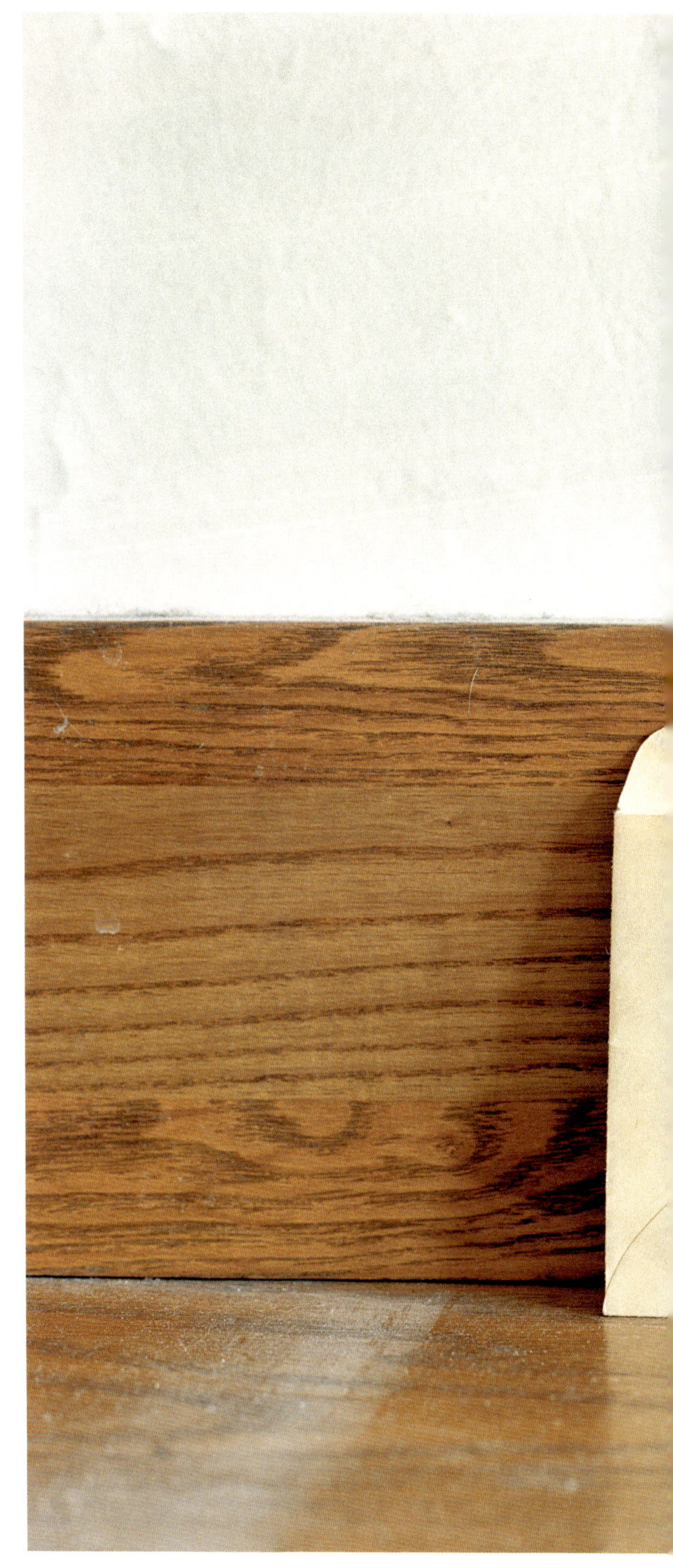

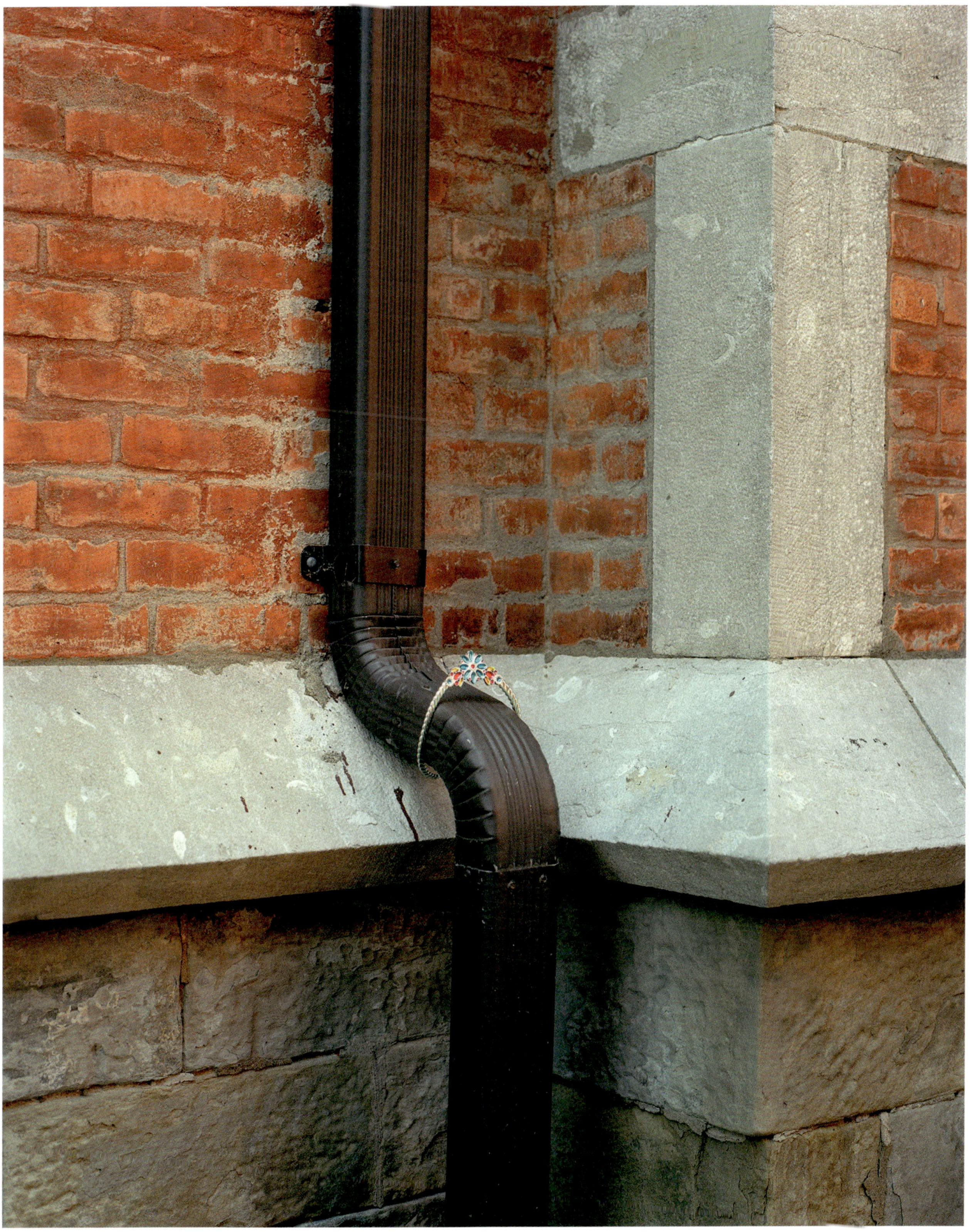

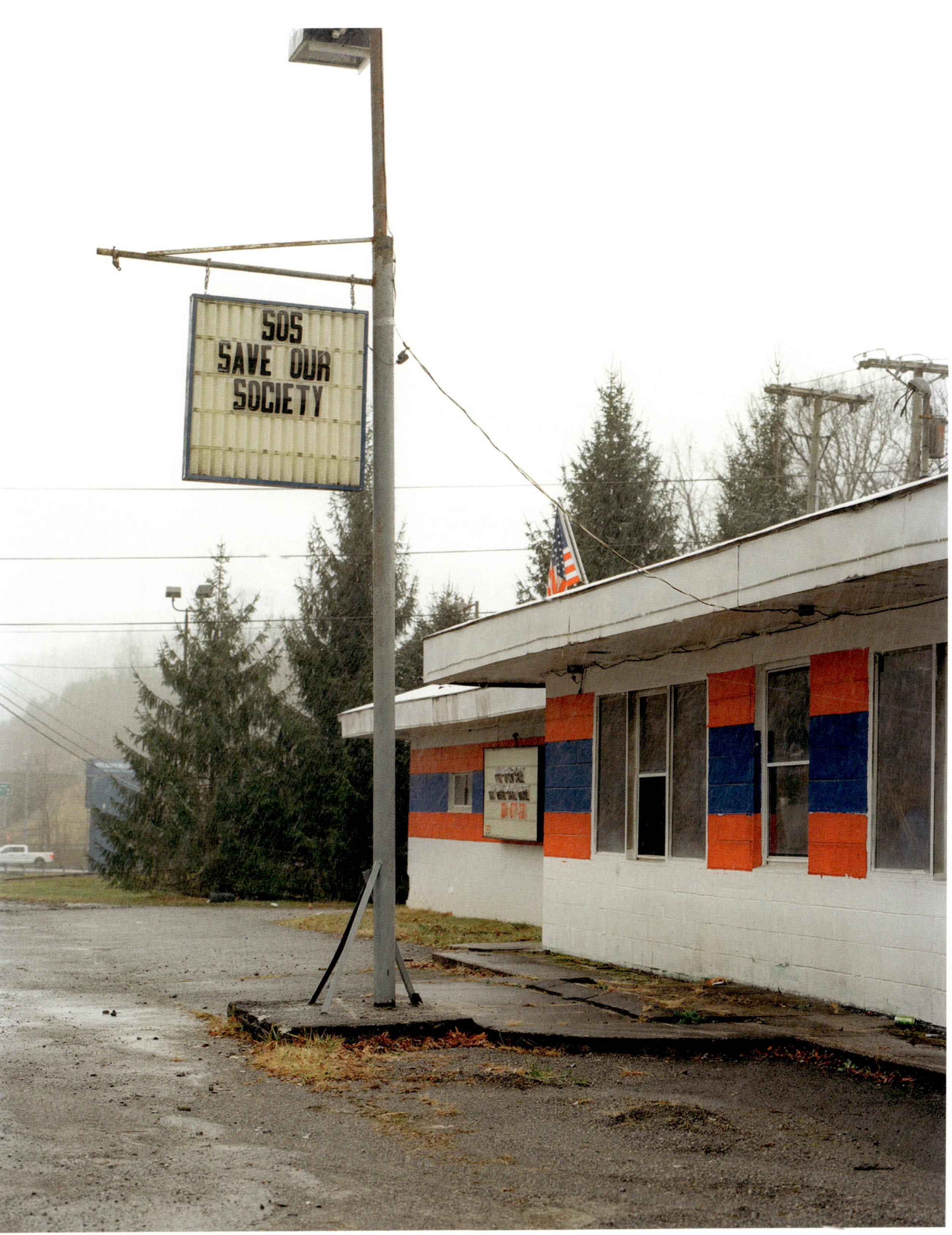
SOS
SAVE OUR
SOCIETY

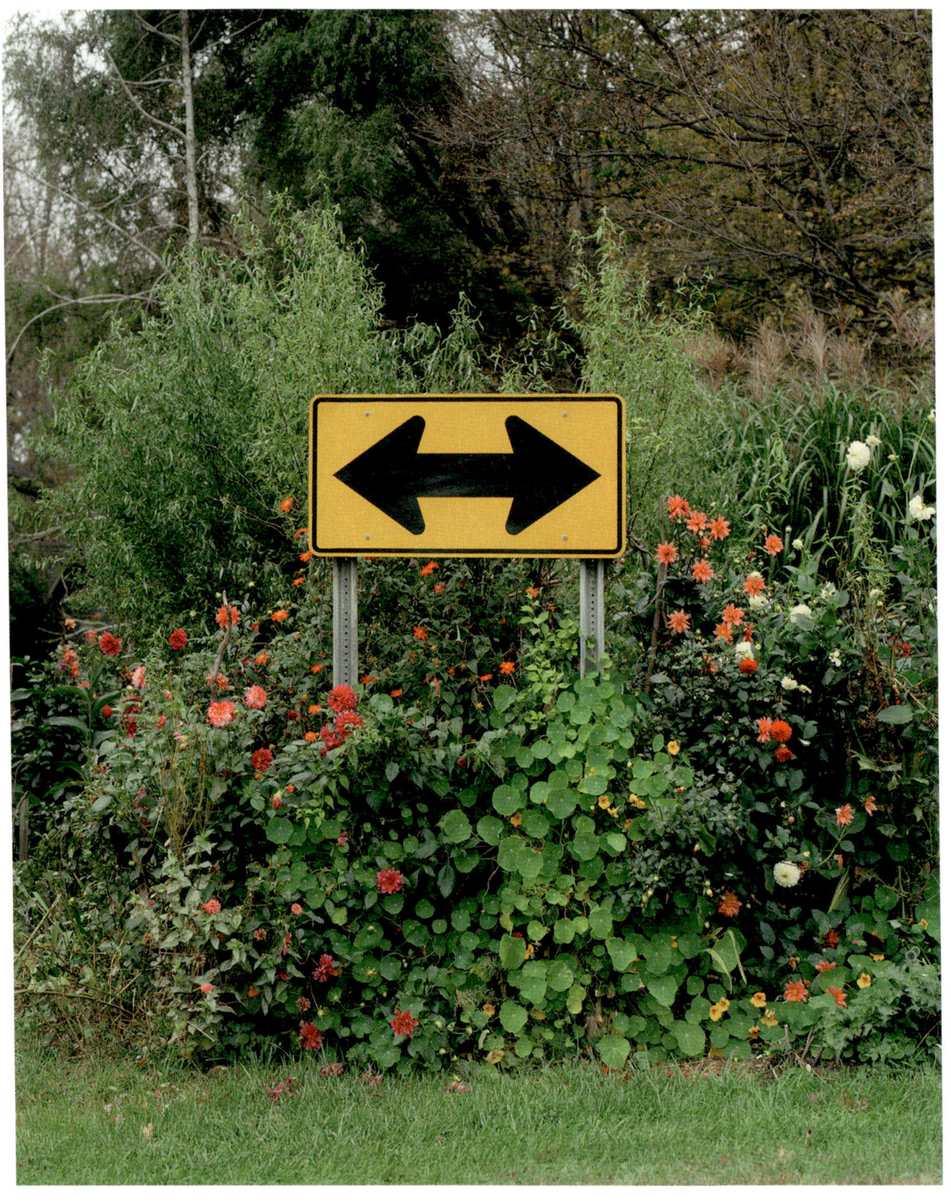

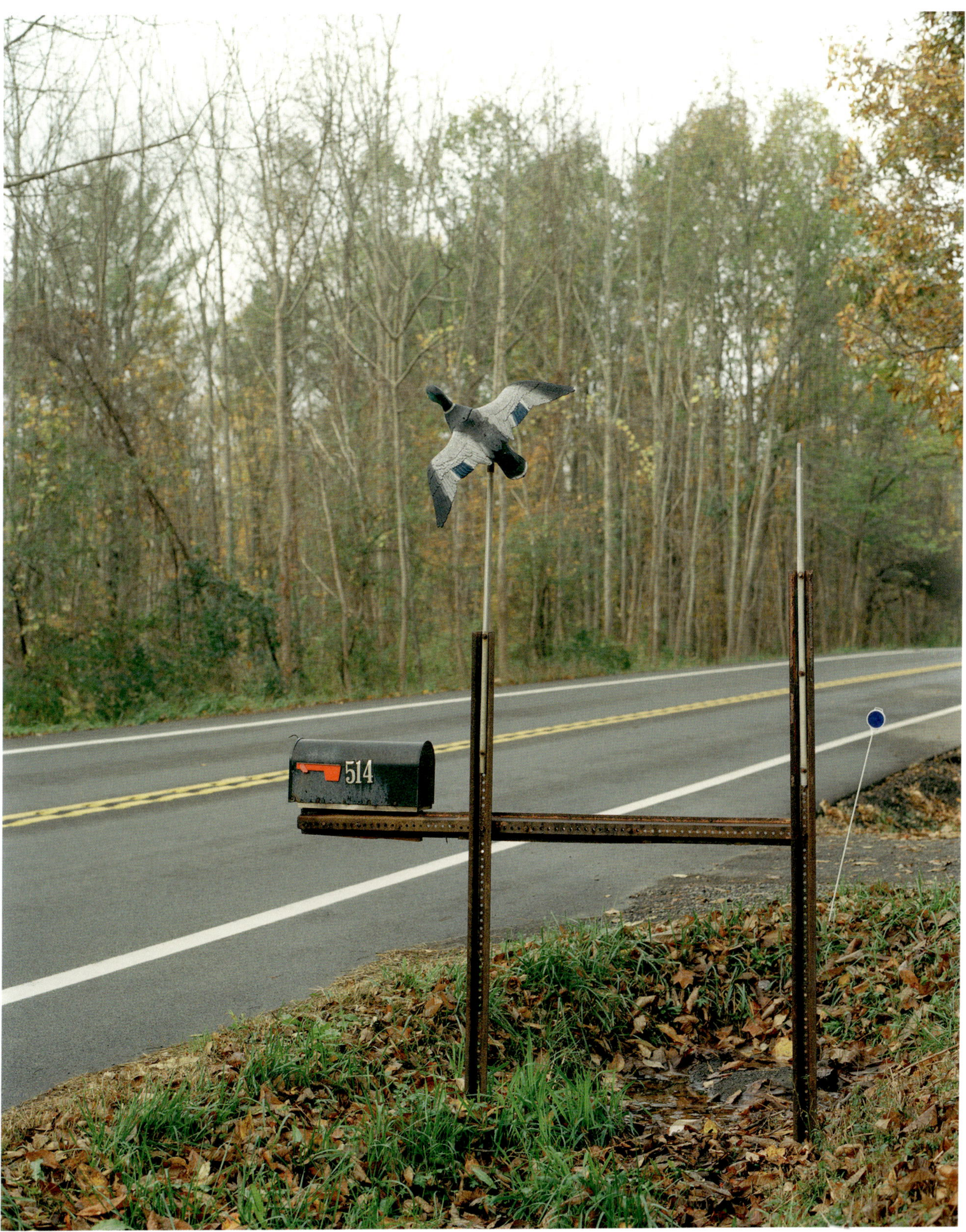
514

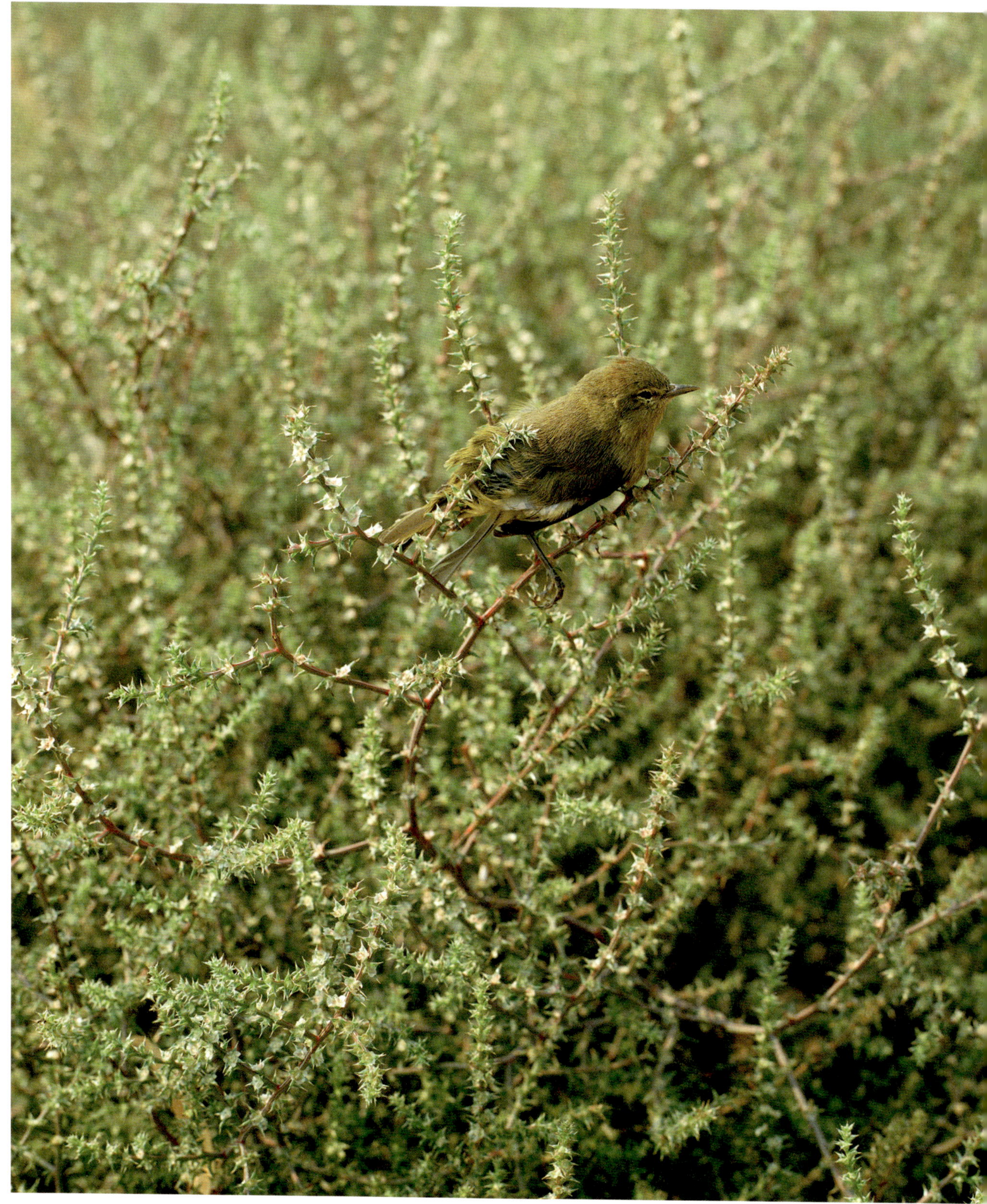

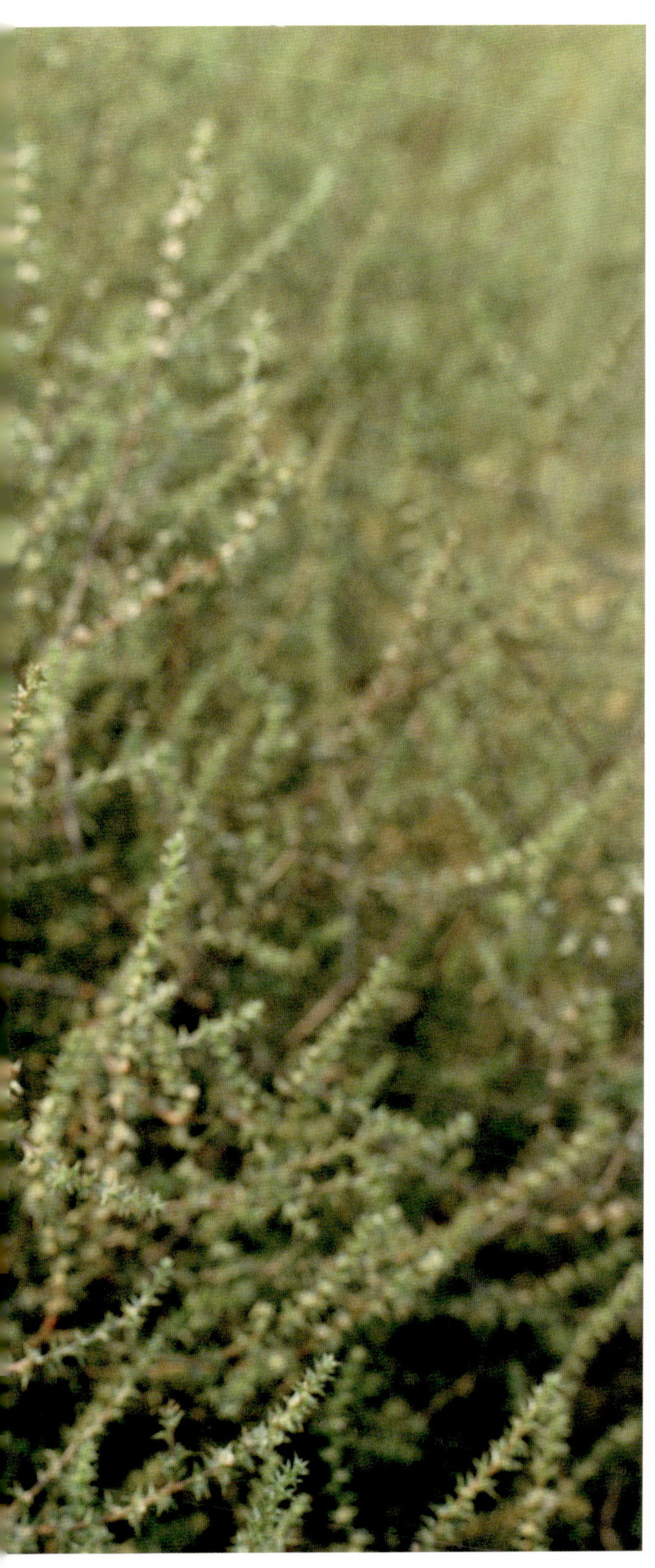

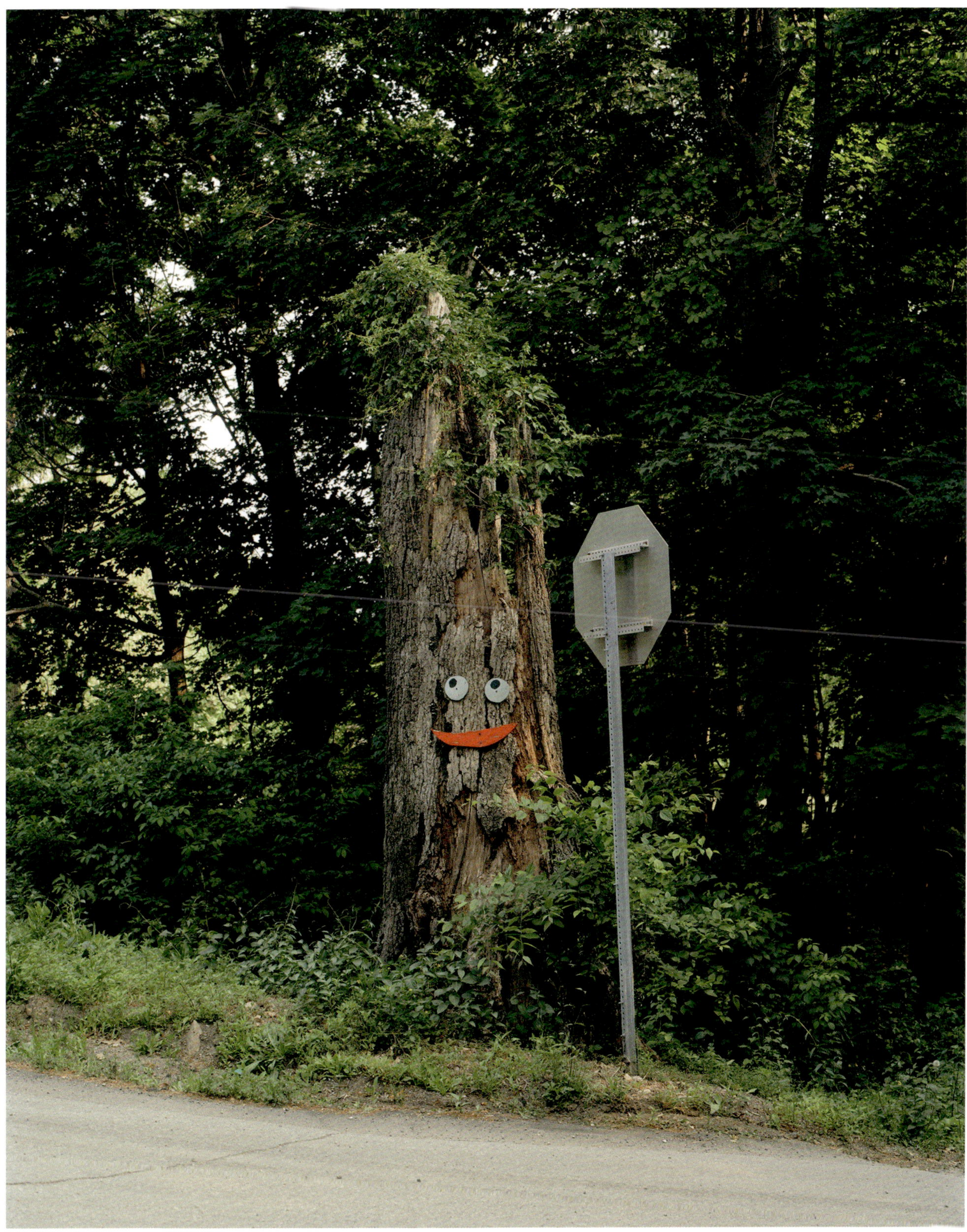

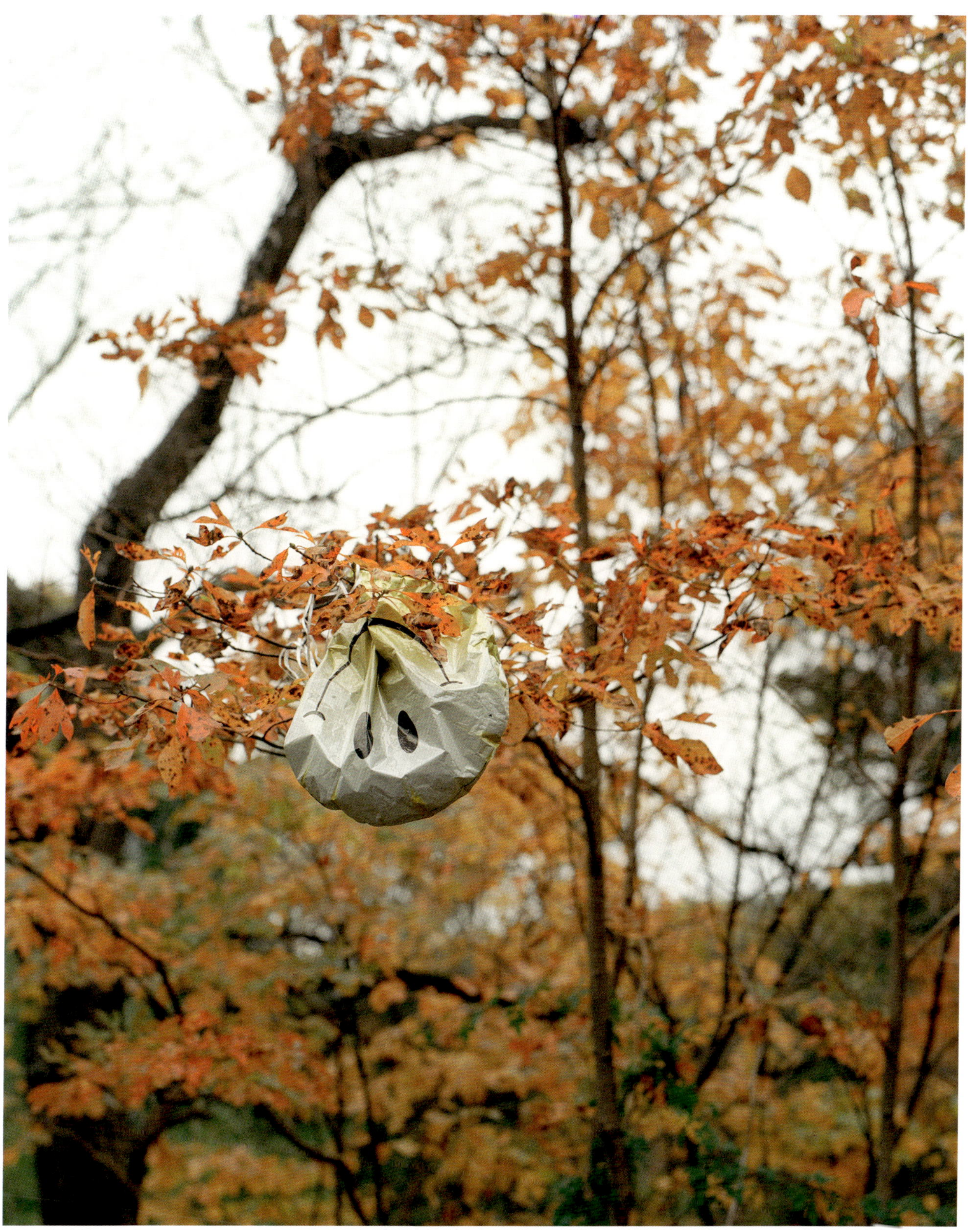

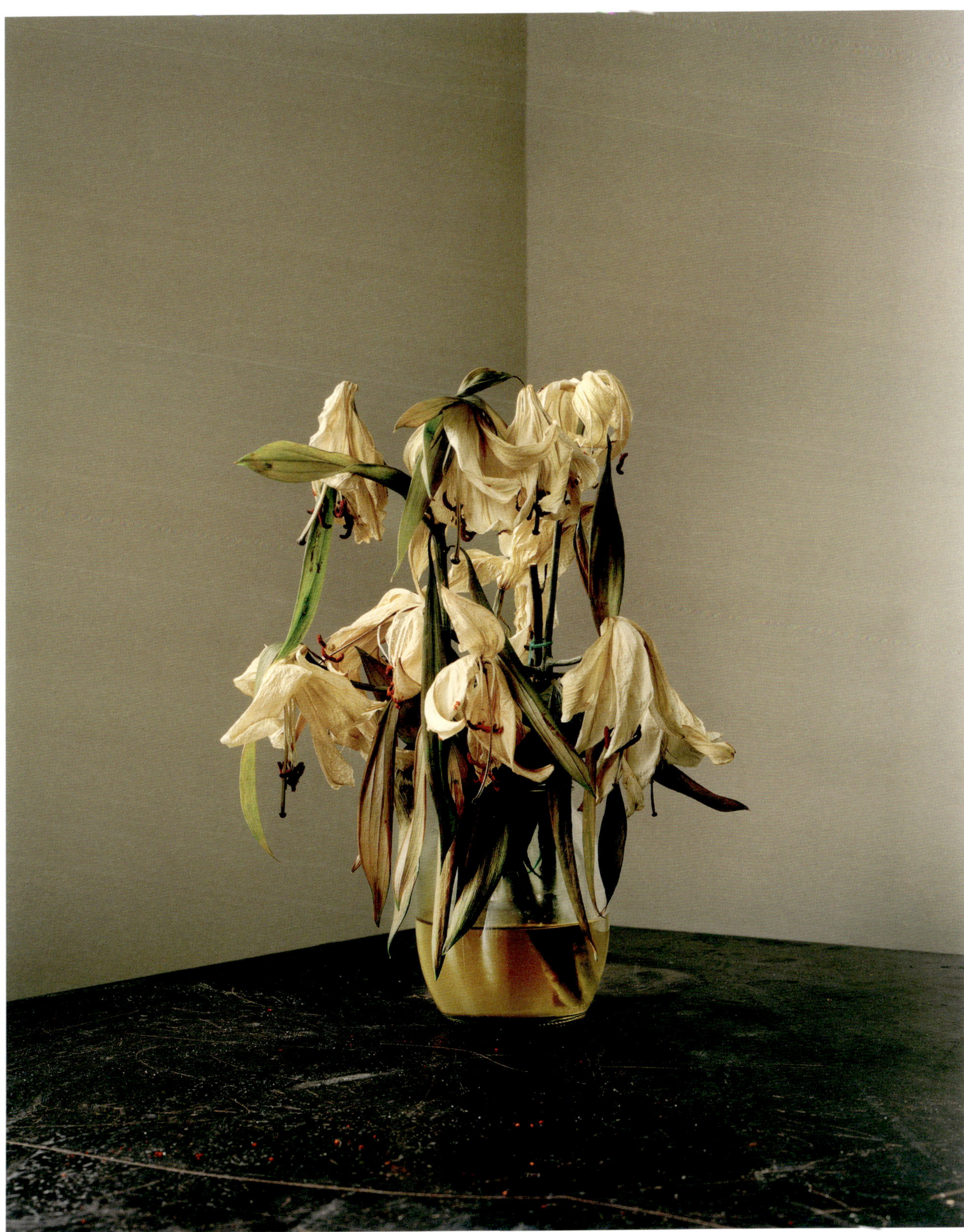

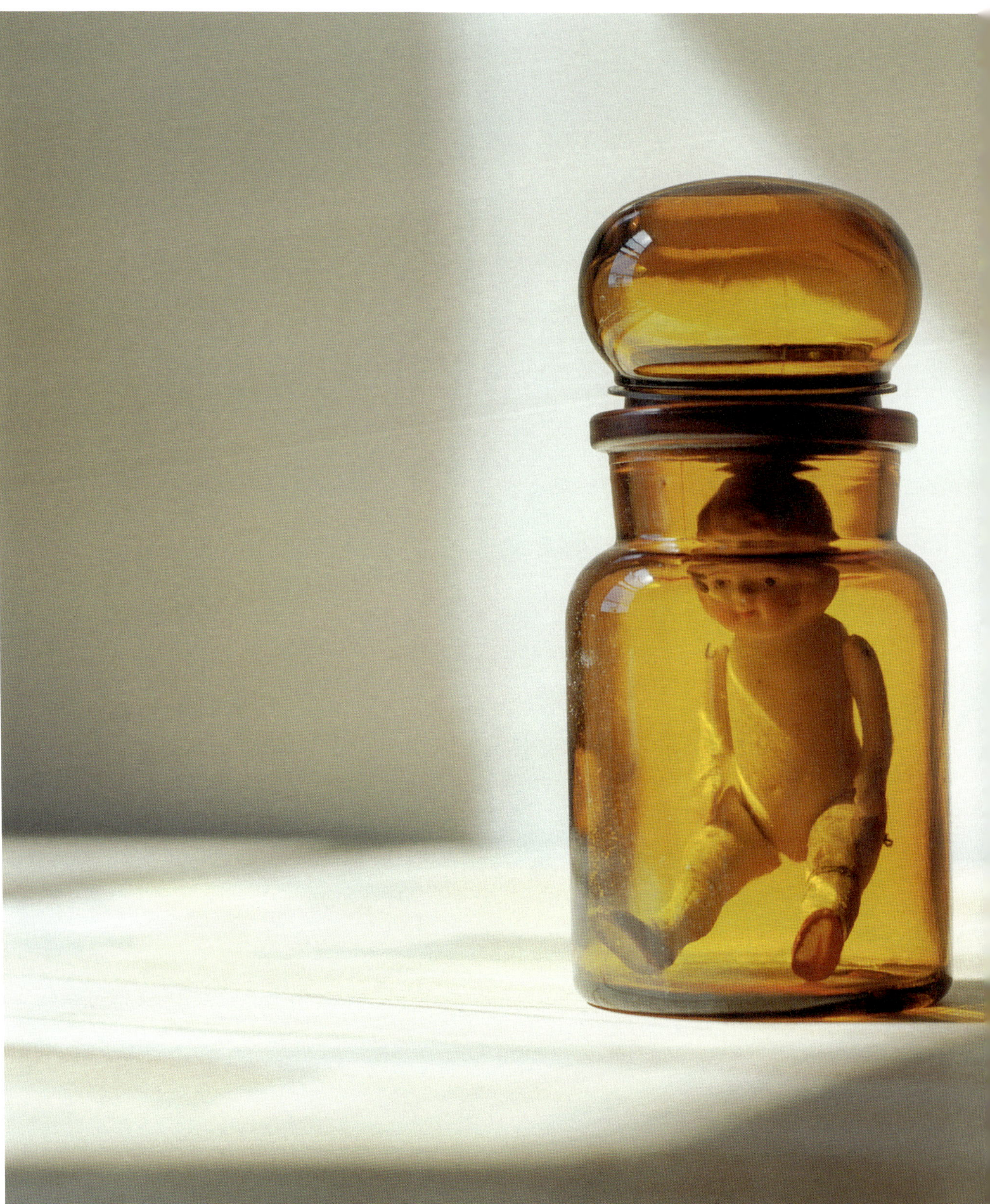

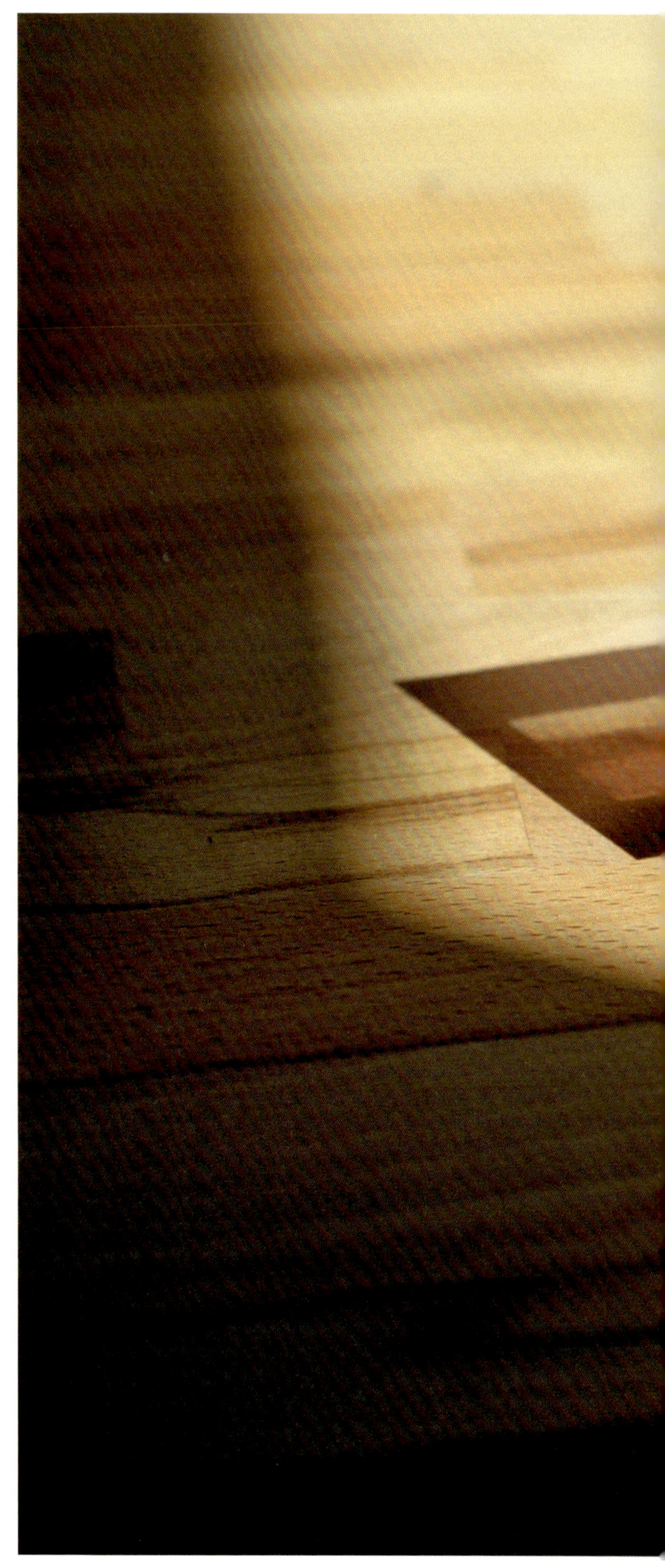

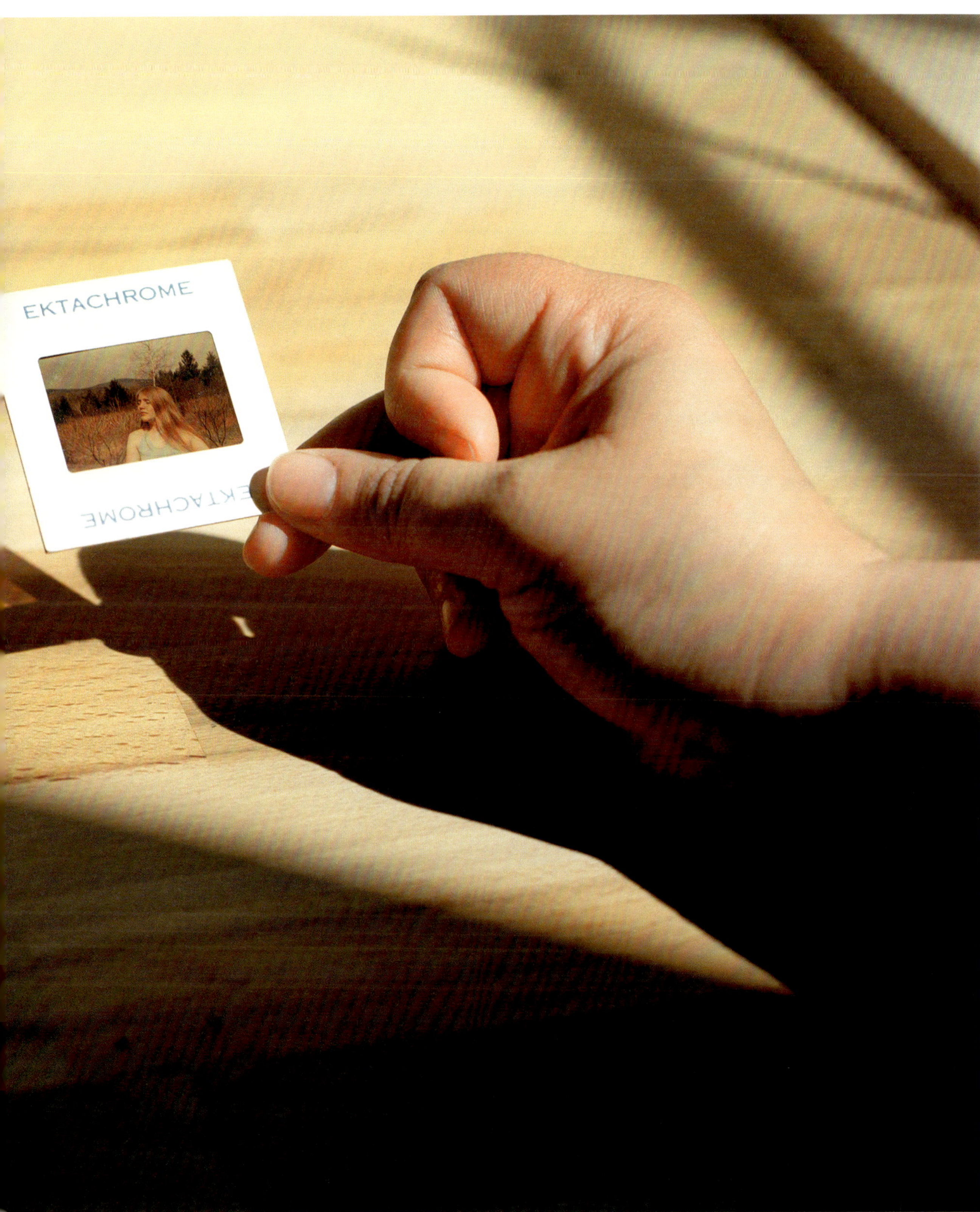
EKTACHROME

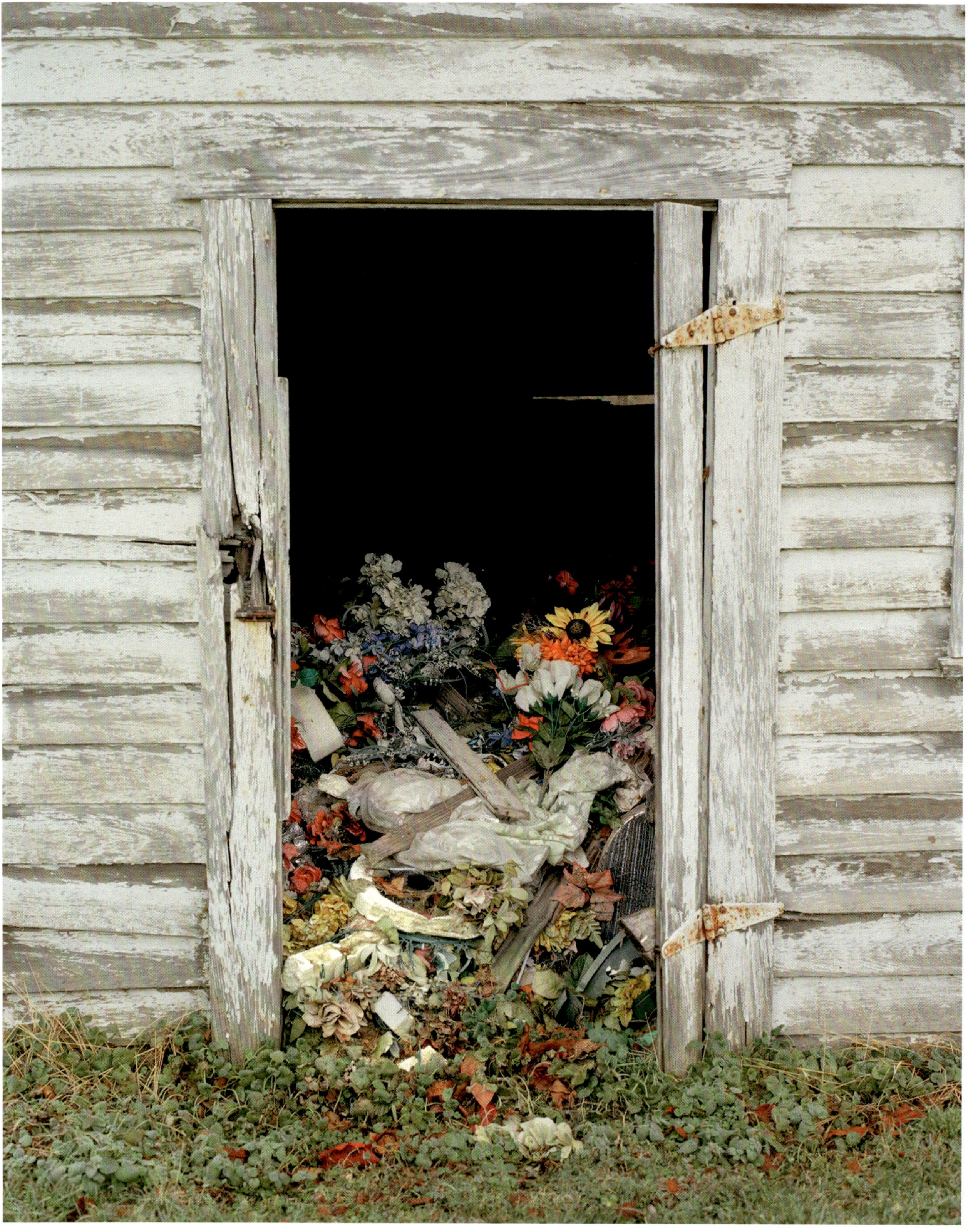

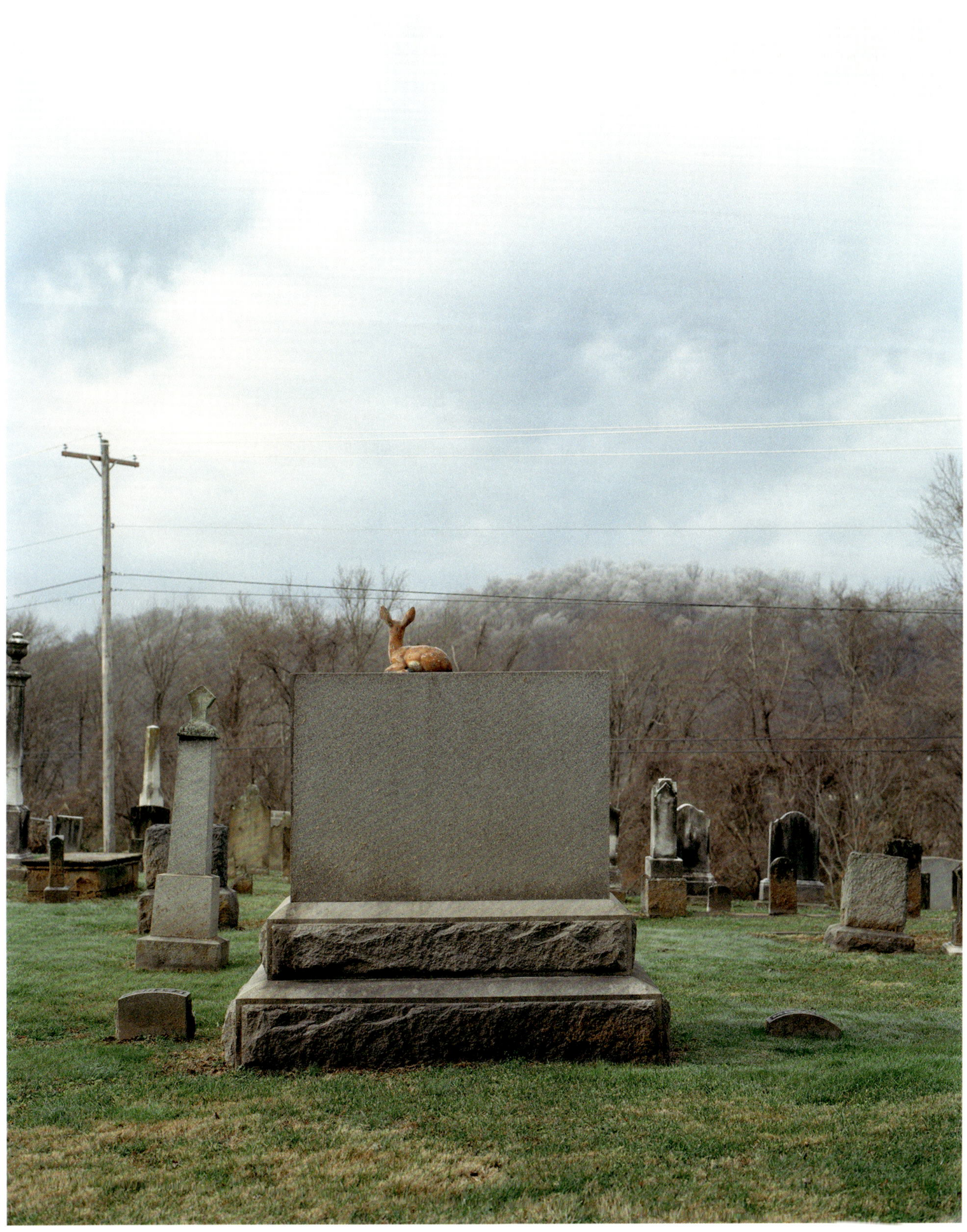

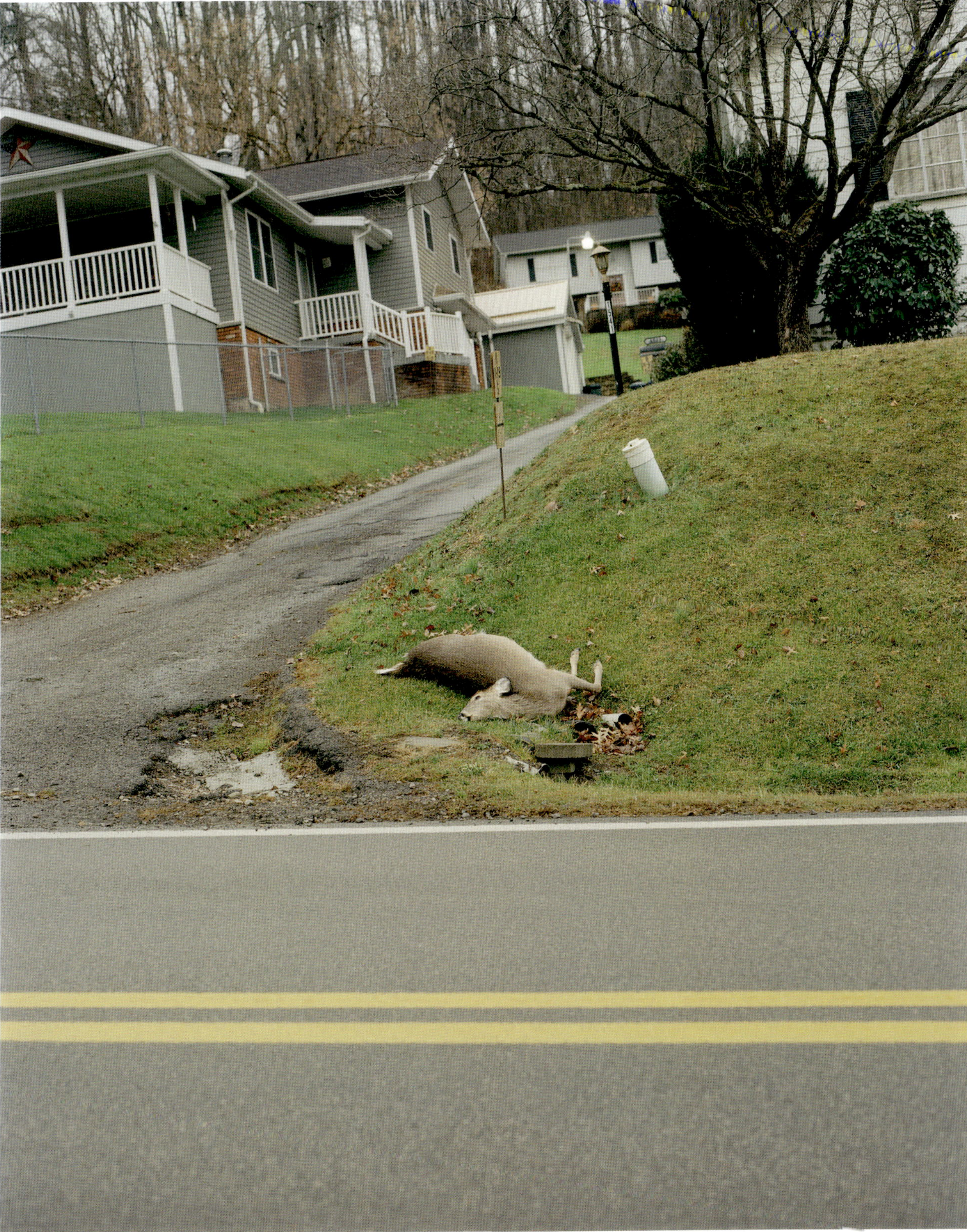

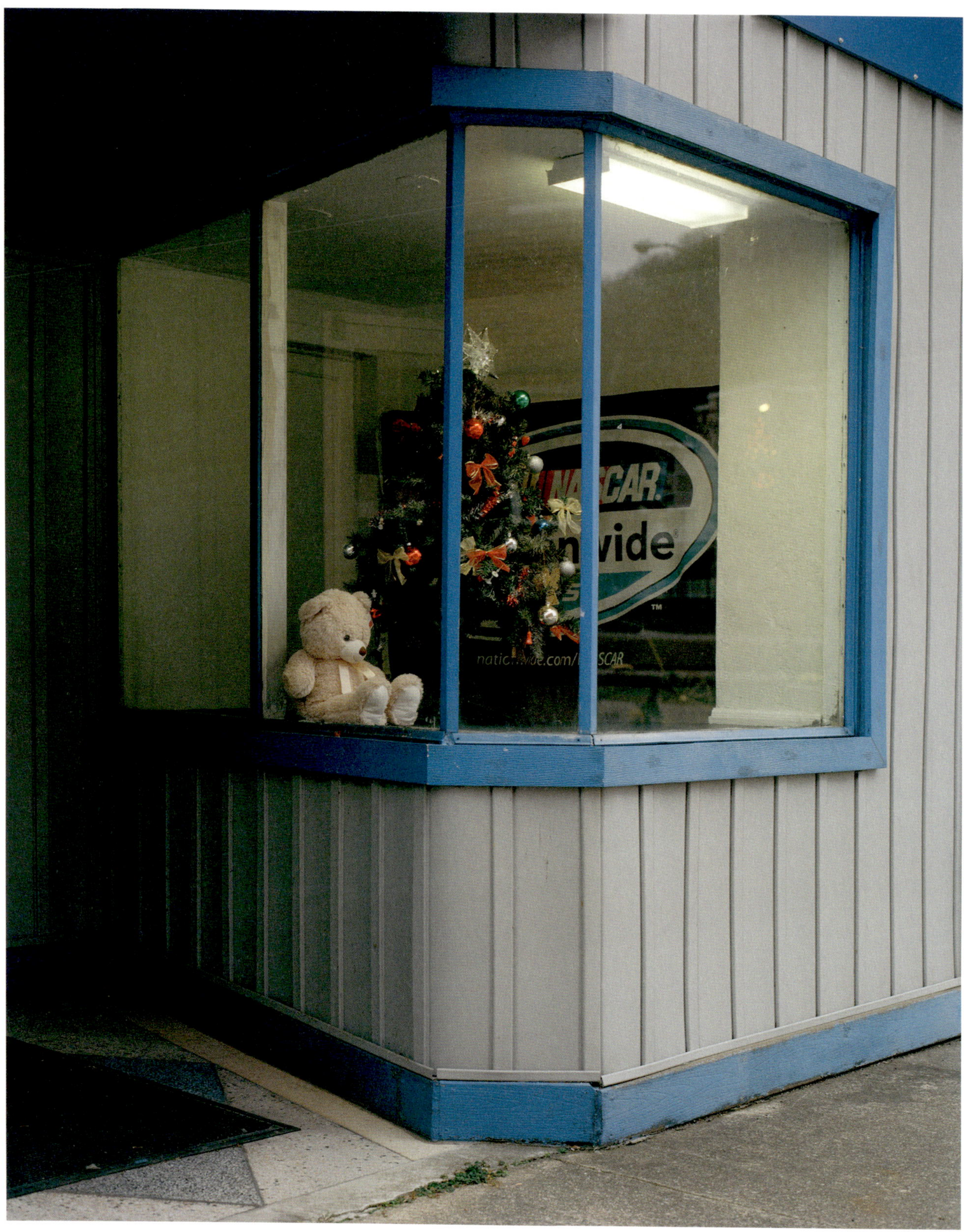
NASCAR

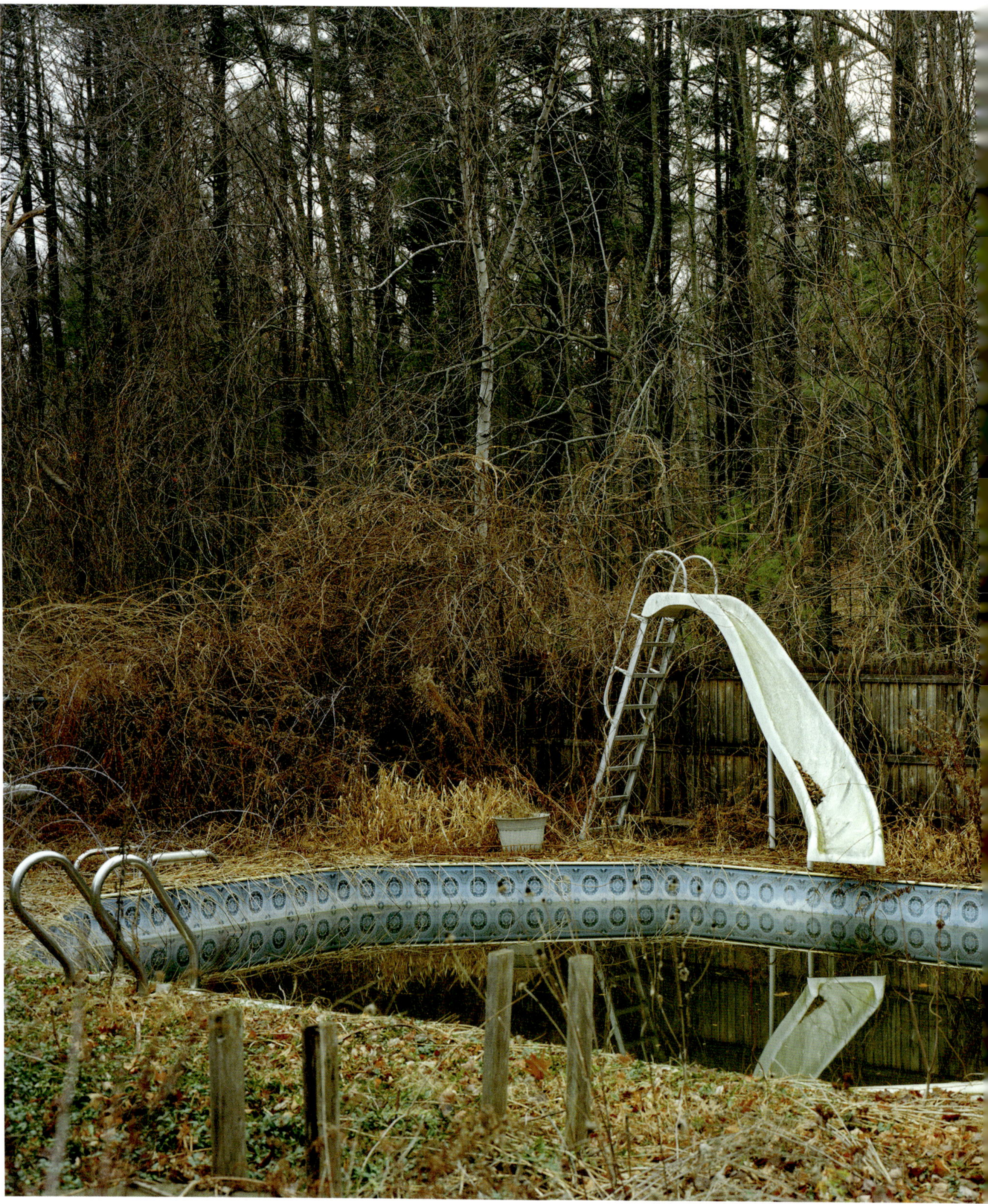

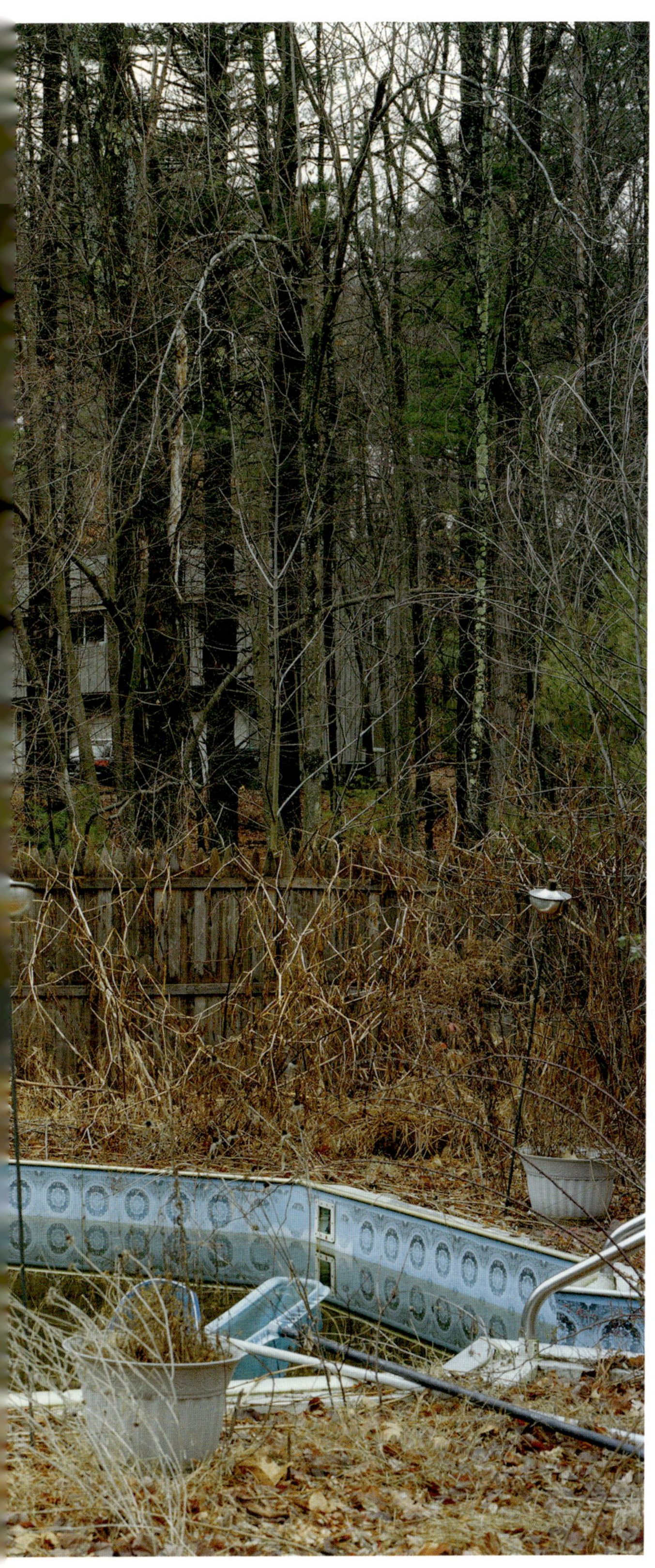

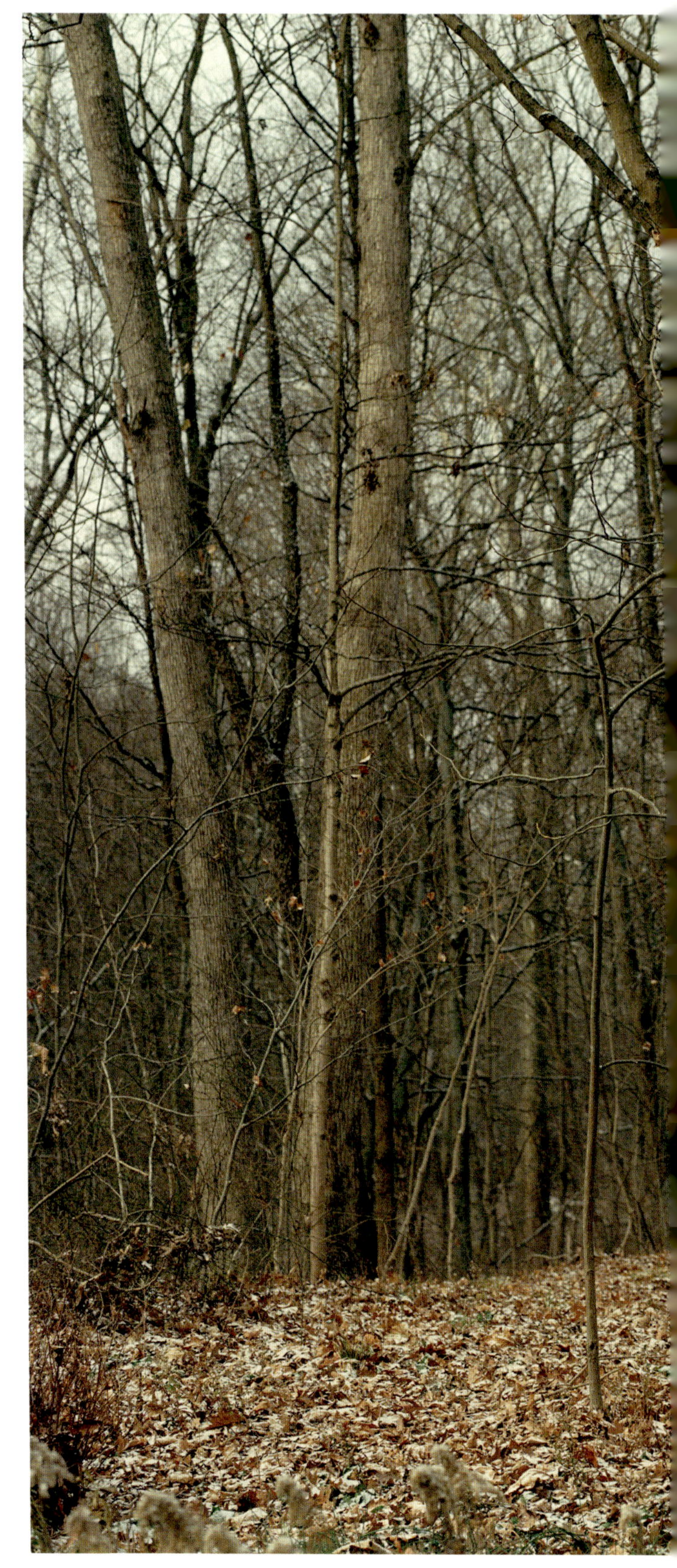

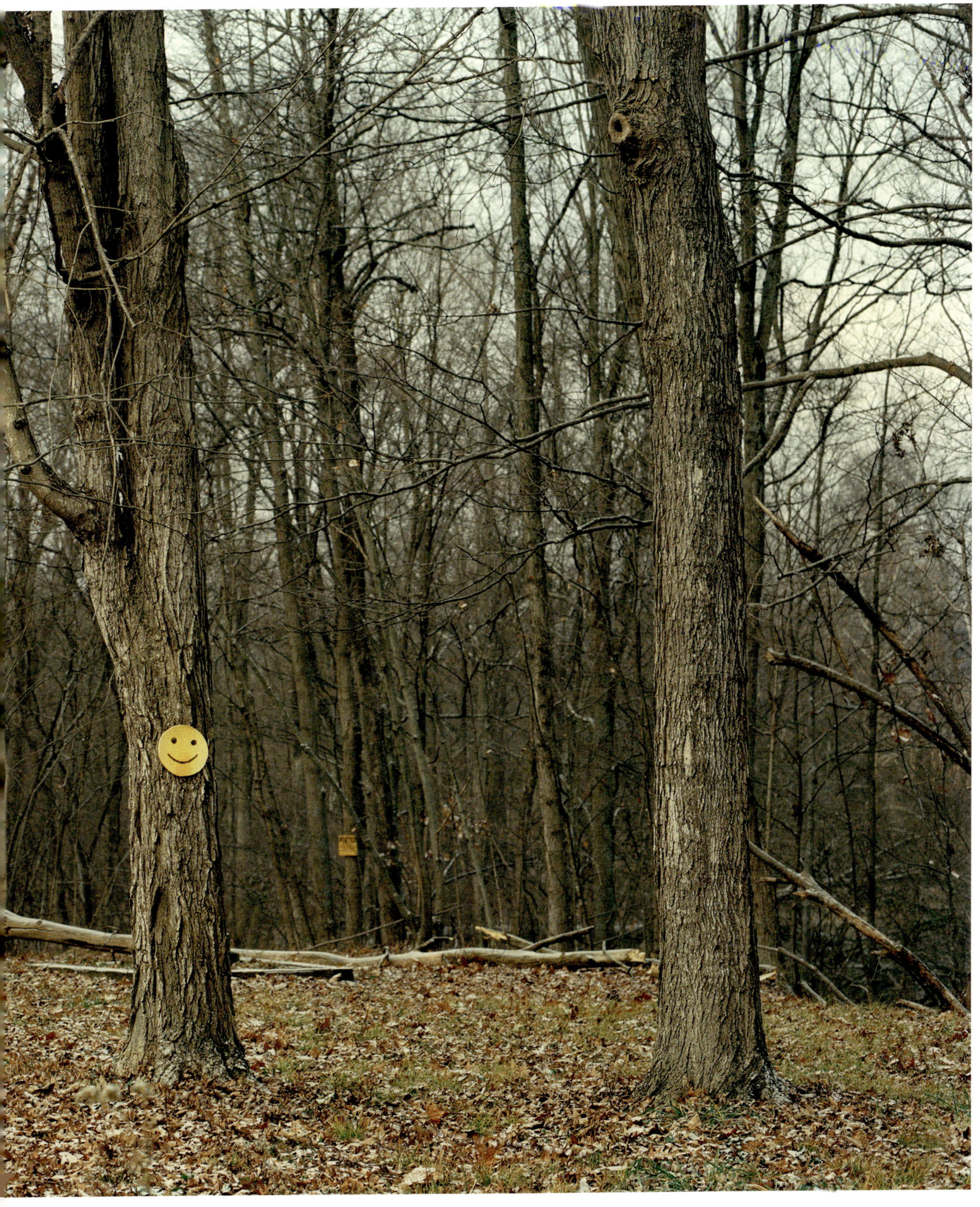

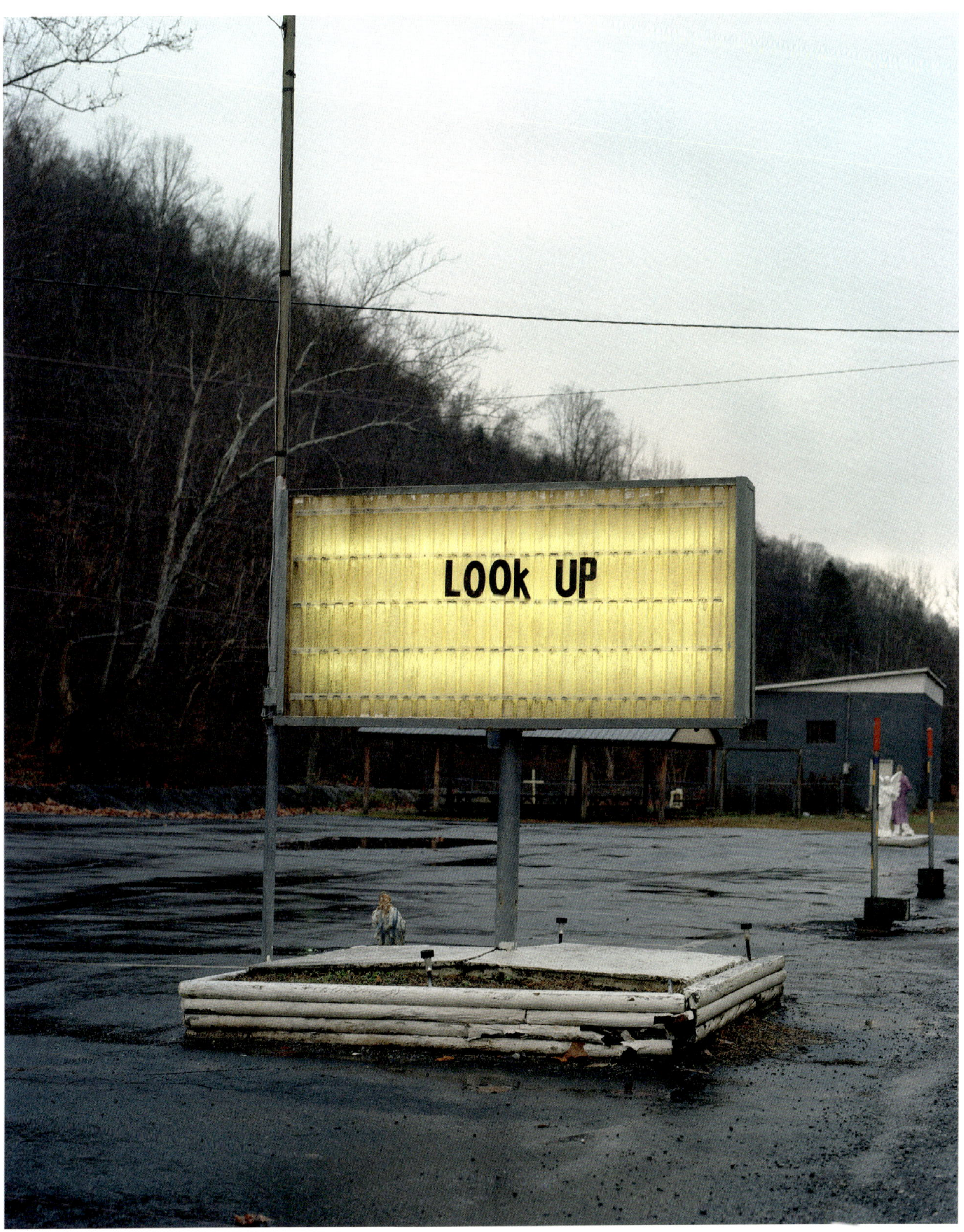
LOOk UP

Tinged with Sadness

It's estimated that almost 280 million people worldwide live with depression. Among this staggering number, this book unveils the personal narrative of just one of them—me.

Why am I sad? Well, perhaps it runs in my blood, a genetic legacy I've inherited. Or maybe it's woven into the complex tapestry of my family fabric. Ironically, it could be the sole bond I share with my mother—a connection tinged with sadness.

My upbringing in a small town, born to immigrant parents, was a kaleidoscope of cultures, languages, and culinary delights. English echoed through the halls of our home, intermingled with the savory aroma of shepherd's pie and the sweet decadence of what my dad called "ding pudding," on account of it being made in a microwave. Yet, beyond our doorstep, Hebrew dominated my interactions at school and with friends. As a child of immigrants, I found myself living in a duality that often left me feeling like an outsider in both worlds. I was a cultural chameleon, navigating the ever-shifting boundaries of identity. Amidst the cacophony of conflicting cultures, there was a profound sense of isolation, a feeling of not quite belonging to either place. It was as if I were adrift in a sea of identities, constantly searching for solid ground amid the shifting tides of self-definition.

In this struggle, solitude became my constant companion. Hours spent alone in my room felt no different from the loneliness that engulfed me in a crowd. Home offered no sanctuary, merely amplifying the stress, anxiety, and, above all, the profound sadness that seemed to permeate every corner. For years my mother has silently battled with clinical depression, navigating its complexities and challenges—an illness that cast a shadow over my youth, though this was something I couldn't fully comprehend at the time. Her struggle became my own, a silent synergy of sadness against the backdrop of everyday life. It took years for me to recognize the impact of her struggles on my own journey through the shadows of melancholy, to understand that her pain was not hers alone, but a legacy passed down through the generations, a burden we both carried in silence and alone.

In the confines of my room, I discovered photography, a medium that allowed me to translate the discord of inner turmoil into visual poetry. Objects ceased to be mere artifacts; they became vessels for unspoken narratives, a language I could speak fluently when words failed me. Through the lens of my camera, I found a voice, a means of expression that transcended the limitations of verbal communication. Each photograph became a window into my soul, a reflection of the inner dialogue I dared not speak aloud. And yet, with all my best intentions, the specter of loneliness and sadness remained, a constant companion hovering at the edge of every frame.

Now, years and thousands of miles away from that bedroom, I find myself grappling with a familiar heaviness, as loneliness and sadness continue to cast a shadow over me. Photography, once a beacon of solace, has taken on a new shape—that of both a savior and tormentor. In the early days, capturing moments through my lens provided a sense of purpose, a lifeline, but as the years passed, photography morphed from a source of comfort into a burden I carried on my shoulders. The need to photograph became a relentless demand. In moments of respite, when I dared to set aside my camera, anxiety crept in like a thief in the night. And yet, even when I yielded to the call and pressed the shutter release, the resulting images bore the weight of the cloud of sadness that hovered above me. It was as if I could no longer escape the grip of sadness, even in the moments when I felt the relief of taking a photo.

Oddly enough, over the past few years, I've stumbled upon countless smile faces in the most unexpected and bizarre places. Whether in the solemn quiet of a graveyard, amidst the dense foliage of a forest, or boldly plastered on driveways, highways, and mailboxes, they appear almost as if the universe is purposefully teasing and daring my sadness. These once cheerful symbols, promising joy, optimism, and hope, take on a sinister tone when taken out of context, transforming into grim reflections of the person behind the lens. With their exaggerated grins and innocent gaze, they radiate happiness in the most brazen and vexing manner imaginable, mocking me and serving as a constant reminder. Yet I find myself capturing them, trapping their false joy in the frame, a stark contrast to the melancholy that envelops me.

Why am I always sad? I find myself grappling with this question, yet the answer remains elusive and I feel no compulsion to provide one. It simply exists, and perhaps accepting that is more than is needed. These images serve as something of a personal odyssey, a journey through the maze that is my relationship with the medium—a mirror that captures the world through my camera's lens, as I try to find answers to these questions. Each photograph is a testament to the complexity of human emotion, a reminder that beauty and sadness often walk hand in hand along the winding paths of our voyage through life.

This is my sadness. It is possible these words will find resonance within you, and if not, perhaps these images will echo louder than any written sentiment.

Dana Stirling

Index

To Yoav, my guiding light amidst the shadows, the sunshine through the clouds of sadness. Thank you for years of love, support, inspiration and dare I say—happiness.

Photographs and Text: Dana Stirling
Copy Editing: Philip Thomas
Project Management: Kehrer Verlag (Sylvia Ballhause)
Design: Kehrer Design (Nicole Gehlen)
Cover Illustration: Elisha Zepeda with use of icon
by ValGraphic/adobe.stock.com
Image Processing: Kehrer Design (Erik Clewe)
Production Management: Kehrer Design (Tom Streicher)

Bibliographic information published by the
Deutsche Nationalbibliothek
The Deutsche Nationalbibliothek lists this publication
in the Deutsche Nationalbibliografie;
detailed bibliographic data is available on the
Internet at https://dnb.dnb.de.

Printed and bound in Germany
ISBN 978-3-96900-159-2

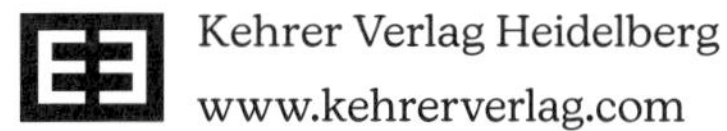